An Illustrated Guide to Consciousness for Kids

Get a clue about your inner self.
Learn to win the battle between
your ego monsters by becoming a
consciousness
superhero!

Dedicated to Grace, Sean, Izzy

My little geniuses, my beautiful vision seekers,
you are my heart.

With this book, I am with you always and forever.
You are Clueberry Warriors.
Don't ever forget to question your fear.

STATE OF MIND

LICENSE TO SUCCEED

NAME: YOU

ADDRESS: HERE

ISSUED: NOW

EXPIRES: NEVER

ISBN: 978 - 0 - 615 - 43816 - 0

Welcome to Clueberry World, a treasure map of your mind!

In your hands is a guidebook and map of Clueberry World, a place that helps you explore your inner world. You are about to experience a treasure map unlike any other map you've ever seen. Yes, it has states. However, the states on this map are called States of Mind. The States of Mind are connected by a train of thought. In this book, you will learn how to navigate your own train of thought. Find out how tricky ego monsters are trying to derail your thoughts and what you can do about it! This book will start you on the path to becoming a consciousness superhero. Clueberry World takes you on a journey, the journey of becoming a vision seeker or "One who sees the way!"

Table of Contents

How To Use This Book

- ⬭ Reading in order is suggested but not necessary

- ⬭ Follow the Clueberry map on the next page as you go

- ⬭ Apply these lessons and characters to your own life

- ⬭ Use this book as a reference guide

- ⬭ Interpret the suggestions so they work for you

- ⬭ Practice developing your Clueberry powers daily

THE CLUEBERRY MAP: Explore States of Mind...

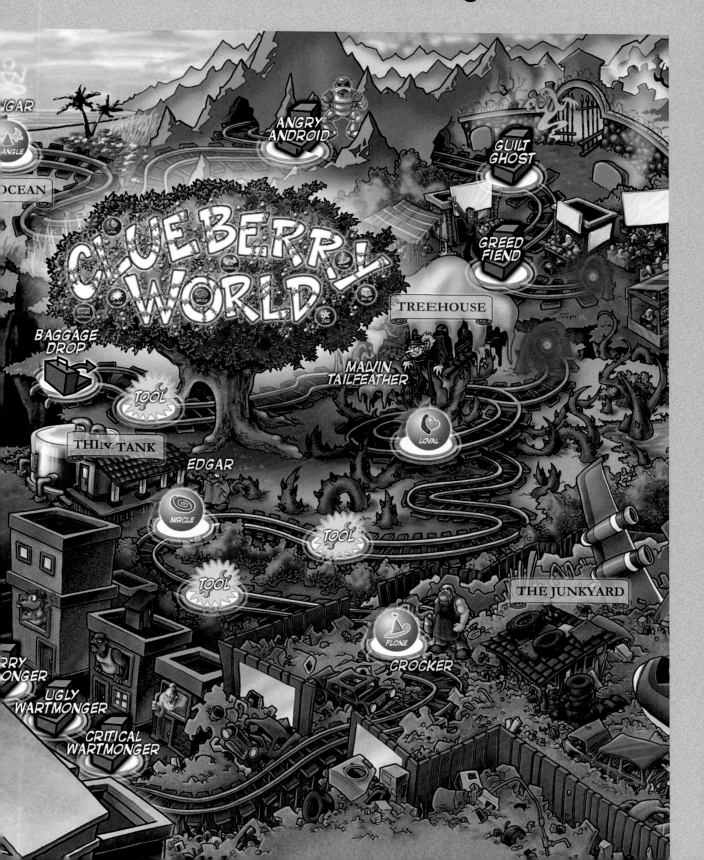

...travel your Train of Thought!

You are the Train.

Welcome aboard! With this book you will embark on a journey that will empower you to understand the 3 biggest questions in life:

Who am I? Where am I going? Why do I feel derailed?

This is Clueberry World, a world that teaches you about the journey within. The very first exciting lesson you need to know? Notice the train tacks run throughout Clueberry World and yet there is no train...well, that's because YOU are the train. You are the conductor of your own train of thought. This means by learning to choose your thoughts, you can have complete control over the direction of your life AND it means if you get derailed in life, you can always get back on track.

Now that you know you are the train, the question is: how do you direct your train of thought? How do you know which way to turn? That question is at the core of every one of us on this planet and in this book you are going to learn how to master being the conductor of your own train of thought.

Let's FIRST talk about where your whole journey starts.

Lesson 2

The Think Tank is your mind.

The journey within begins at the Think Tank! The starting point for the direction of your life begins in your mind. Think of your mind as the train station. Since you are the train, and you can't go anywhere without fuel, this where you receive "fuel" for your journey.

There are 2 kinds of fuel you can choose:

1. positive fuel or positive thoughts: this kind of fuel keeps you on track
2. negative fuel or negative thoughts: this kind of fuel leads to becoming derailed

Here's a big question: how do you choose your fuel? In other words, how do you choose positive thoughts over negative ones?

The answer is: what you pay attention to in your mind will determine your choice. Think about the phrase paying attention.

There truly is a cost for what you pay attention to. If you pay attention to negative thoughts too often, you will find yourself derailed (that's not necessarily a bad thing because being derailed offers great lessons but we will get to that later)!

Your mind operates on two channels.

This is what it looks like inside the Think Tank.

All the little things floating inside are your thoughts.

As you can see, there are lots of shadowy thoughts in your mind. In the next lesson, you'll understand what the illuminated thought in the middle is called.

The dark thoughts are mostly negative and tend to pile up in the corners of your mind in the form of old thought patterns, emotional baggage and lingering fears from bad memories in the past or worries about the future.

Shadowy, dark thoughts are generally very common. But why? Check out the TV metaphor below and you'll get it!

Like a TV, your mind has channels.

When you turn on a TV, there are some channels that come free and there are other channels that you can only receive on your TV if you choose to upgrade. The same goes for your mind!

The free channel or default channel usually broadcasts chronic negative thinking. Basically, this channel is the channel of fear based thinking, often projecting darker or stress causing thoughts like worry, anxiety or doubt.

Just like a TV, you can upgrade and choose which channel you want to put your attention towards. Upgrading means choosing to think positive thoughts. Notice that positive thinking is a choice. You must consciously choose to upgrade your channel of thinking.

A miracle is an illuminated thought.

In Clueberry World, MIRCLE Clueberries represent MIRACLE THOUGHTS.

These are the properties of miracles:

1. miracles are positive thoughts

2. miracles are inspired thoughts

3. they rise up or emerge in your Think Tank

How do we know a miracle thought? Miracle thoughts cause a burst of energy , bring about positive emotions like joy, peace, a sense of purpose, stimulate inspired action and creative ideas and answer the questions:

"Who am I?" and "Where am I going?" in a profound way.

MIRCLE

How to filter out your MIRCLES (miracles)

Miracle thoughts emerge in your mind all the time!

Here's a myth: When you sit in silence, you are not doing anything.

False! The greatest action you can take is to be silent. Why? That's the act of "meditating" or watching your own mind.

Worry, doubt and anxiety are all negative thought forms in your Think Tank, so it's important to not add MORE negative thought forms to your Think Tank while in silence.

This means:

Accept the thoughts you have, even if they are negative. Judging yourself for the thoughts you have gives them even more power. Your mind tends to generate negative thoughts as a default channel, so it's normal to experience negative thoughts, images, or ideas in various forms.

When you sit in silence for a few moments without judging yourself for the thoughts you experience, you are creating space in your mind for all the negative thoughts to lose their grip over you, and they begin to disappear naturally.

The relief that emerges in this inner silence, when the negative thoughts has subsided…cause your MIRACLE thoughts to reveal themselves. Scoop them up and treasure them. They are there to give you guidance!

When you pay attention to your miracle thoughts, you are choosing a path that will lead guid you towards your true purpose, towards the brilliant experience of gaining INSIGHT into your unique voice, your reason for being, and the underlying meaning behind your life.

Lesson 6

Tools are Available to You

Tools help you along by creating a shift in your perception.

Tools:

1. Tools are everywhere along your path.

2. Tools come in surprising shapes and sizes.

3. Tools can only help you if you are willing to see them as tools.

Kinds of tools to discover are:
Wisdom, Compassion, Contentment

Tool Shed

Here are some examples of the tools available to you during your journey:

Confidence Flavored Goo Paste

Directions: Twist cap off
Be prepared for instant turbo blast, aim at yourself or squirt on Doubt Dragon
Upon contact goo freezes sparks of doubt into ice chips
Side Effect: Leaves you oozing with confidence

Worry Thinner

Directions: Pour 3 tablespoons into Worry Wartmonger's Vex to dilute
Cure Your Vex causing distress
Comes with FREE stirrer!

Courage Grenade

with special dual purpose capsules that explode upon impact
Upon impact to its target, release nerve capsules containing Courage powder (will give you the nerve to face anything within a 20 foot radius)
Also reverses your own nerve damage caused by the Anxiety Android turning you into a BasketCase
BONUS: Grenade also explodes the BasketCase exposing what The Anxiety Android doesn't want you know! (That it's always empty!)

TOOL

FLONE

CROCKER

THE JUNKYARD

Begin where you are, even if you're in the Junkyard.

Begin where you are.

Often times, when miracle thoughts arise up within us, we feel ready to conquer the world!

Very quickly, we look around and feel an equally powerful emotion: stuck.

Now, you may think: nothing looks like a miracle is about to unfold!

This is called being in The Junkyard.

This is when you have BIG ideas and visions and goals (your miracle thoughts) and look around and think, "How am I ever going to make this happen?" Usually it's an apparent lack of resources or disadvantages that's causing this feeling of frustration inside you. Whatever the specific details for your life, you are always in The Junkyard for a reason: this is where you learn the power of the Flone Clueberry.

Identify the Junk.

So you are in The Junkyard.

Sometimes, circumstances exist to teach us something or challenge us to grow in a very specific way, such as in the direction of greater self love by releasing blame for how you've been hurt by another or to develop a character quality like bravery or to force you to become better at practicing forgiveness.

When it comes to living in alignment with your purpose, the biggest commitment you can make is realizing what junk is surrounding you and learning to detach from that junk by seeing it for the lesson that is hiding inside it. So, what is junk? Junk can be:

- *friends* that don't support, uplift or inspire you

- negative *ideas* about yourself such as rumors that other people created about YOU that you have adopted as true without realizing it (and are living up to, even)

- family *relationships* that keep you in a role that you have loooong outgrown

- *statements* from teachers in school that created a self image such as "I am not good at writing," or "I am terrible at art."

- *memories* leaking the power you have to move onward and upward on your path

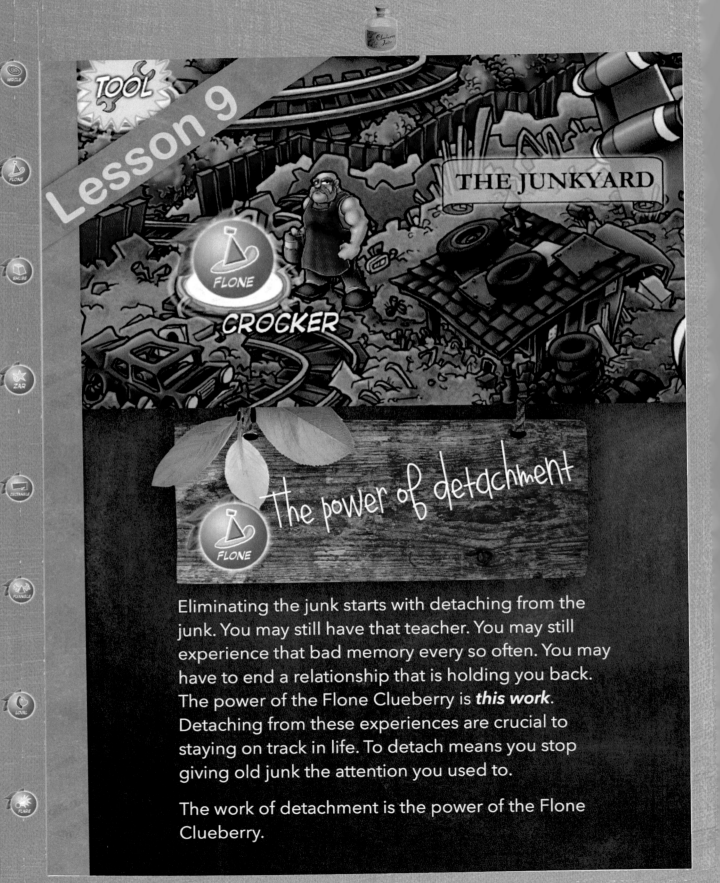

TOOL

THE JUNKYARD

FLONE

CROCKER

FLONE

The power of detachment

Eliminating the junk starts with detaching from the junk. You may still have that teacher. You may still experience that bad memory every so often. You may have to end a relationship that is holding you back. The power of the Flone Clueberry is **this work**. Detaching from these experiences are crucial to staying on track in life. To detach means you stop giving old junk the attention you used to.

The work of detachment is the power of the Flone Clueberry.

How does detachment work? Think of your attention as a currency.

Remember that whatever you pay attention to literally has a cost. You are either investing IN or paying for negative results OR if you are focused on the positive, your attention is paying for positive results and feelings. When you STOP paying attention to your junk, your junk has less power over you and will STOP bothering you. You have to stop paying. You just stop. That doesn't mean you don't stand up for what's right or true fearing it's negative. The truth is not negative. You have to be honest and honesty is positive, even if to others it feels negative. Fill up your time with seeking positive people, uplifting mentors and creative endeavors. Keep practicing detachment from negative experiences and people until they no longer bother you. This is how you stop investing in negative results for yourself. When you are tempted to pay attention to your old junk, remember that the payoff is BIG for staying detached.

With detachment, you are literally making an investment in staying on track with your empowered path, a path that leads to actual experiences that support and ONLY celebrate the best in you. Detachment is literally worth its weight in gold.

Anchor your Attention in the Present Moment.

This is called an Attention Anchor.

Paying attention is the most important aspect of living on purpose and in alignment with your empowered path.

Learning to pay attention is NOT EASY. This is because your Think Tank is cluttered with so many useless thoughts and if you remember the image of the TV, your mind's default channel can be like a 24 hour rerun of a series playing out a lot of negativity.

Often, our minds will automatically flip back to negativity without realizing it. The Attention Anchor represents all this 'awareness' work happens in the PRESENT MOMENT. Use this image to train yourself to attune yourself. See yourself grounded with your mind illuminated.

Choosing to be aware and to continually turn your inner dial back to the upgraded channel in each and every moment is the most important ACTION you can take. Awareness is an action!

Anchor your attention in the present moment to stay in tune with upgraded thinking!

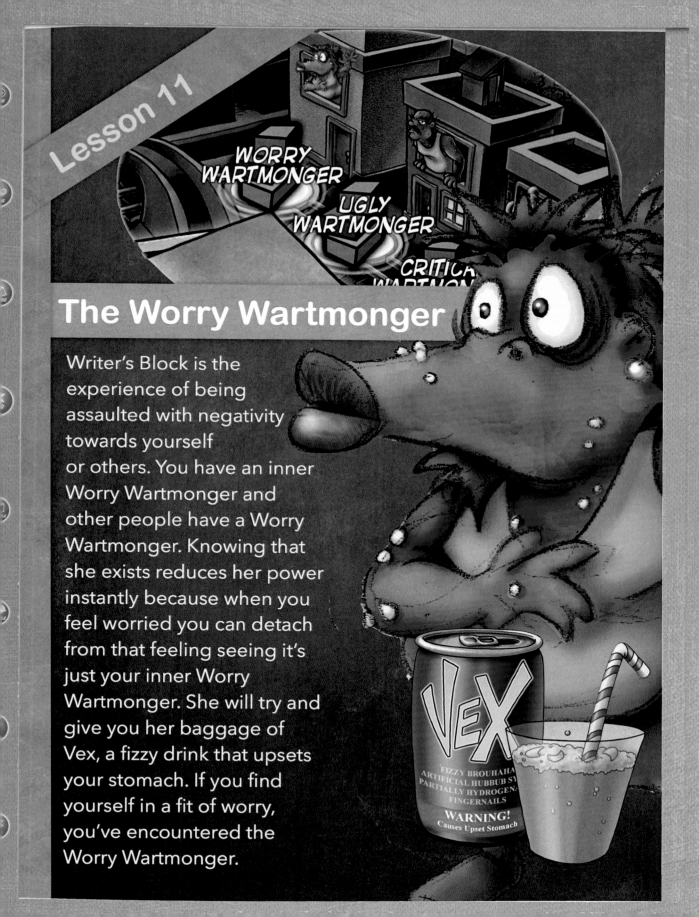

WORRY WARTMONGER

UGLY WARTMONGER

CRITICA WARTMON

The Worry Wartmonger

Writer's Block is the experience of being assaulted with negativity towards yourself or others. You have an inner Worry Wartmonger and other people have a Worry Wartmonger. Knowing that she exists reduces her power instantly because when you feel worried you can detach from that feeling seeing it's just your inner Worry Wartmonger. She will try and give you her baggage of Vex, a fizzy drink that upsets your stomach. If you find yourself in a fit of worry, you've encountered the Worry Wartmonger.

VEX

FIZZY BROUHAHA
ARTIFICIAL HUBBUB SY
PARTIALLY HYDROGEN.
FINGERNAILS

WARNING!
Causes Upset Stomach

The Ugly Wartmonger

You will face ignorance in yourself by facing your limitations and also in others who will assault you with their limitations in ugly ways. Encountering the Ugly Wartmonger in yourself or in another feels like you've been injected with something toxic. Knowing and recognizing the face of ignorance helps you not be so effected by encountering the pain of ignorance. We all have an inner Ugly Wartmonger. Some show up in harsher and nastier ways than others.

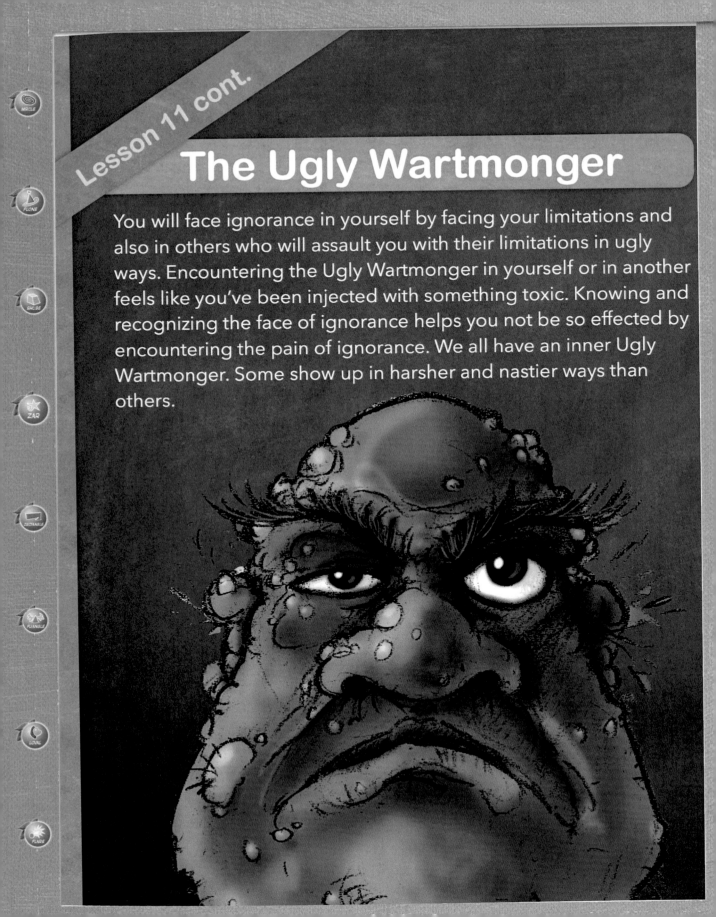

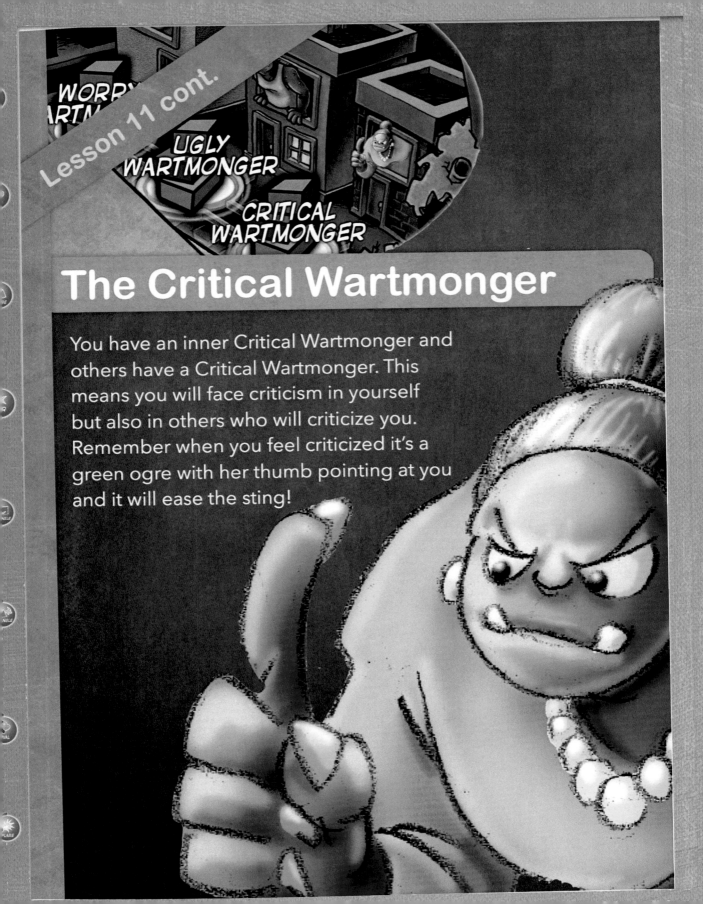

WORRY
ARTM...

UGLY
WARTMONGER

CRITICAL
WARTMONGER

The Critical Wartmonger

You have an inner Critical Wartmonger and others have a Critical Wartmonger. This means you will face criticism in yourself but also in others who will criticize you. Remember when you feel criticized it's a green ogre with her thumb pointing at you and it will ease the sting!

What Baggage are you carrying?

We carry emotional baggage from encounters with these inner monsters. For instance, if you feel DEGRADED, you are carrying around a D Grade Carp from the Critical Wartmonger. You've been BELITTLED and this means YOU let the criticism get to you. What if believing the critic meant you had to carry around a smelly, rotten fish that constantly played "Don't Worry Be Little"? Hanging on to criticism is like having to carry around a smelly, rotten fish that plays a belittling tune over and over. Drop it!

Vex is another word for worry. Worry upsets your stomach and is filled with artificial ingredients. This means that most of what you are worrying about is based in fear, which is a false perception of the truth. Worrying about the past or the future takes you out of the present moment, which is the ONLY place where you can control your life (the only point in time that is REAL). Drop the Vex baggage by refusing to give attention to the Worry Wartmonger in yourself and others.

What Baggage are you carrying?

Have you ever felt poisoned? If so, then the Ugly Wartmonger really got to you! The Ugly Wartmonger represents toxicity. Some people and thoughts are toxic. This means that no matter which way you look at it, you feel contaminated by the experience of that person or the thought. All this means is at this point, you are not ready to deal with the situation. It's time to let it be or just stay away.

Ignorance is harsh and can leave you feeling wounded. Soothe yourself by lathering up in contentment. How?

AFFIRM:
I can choose to be content instead of this.

Baggage is real. We really do carry its weight.

You may not realize it, but you are carrying an invisible backpack through your life. Inside this invisible backpack is your baggage.

When you are not aware of how you deal with the negative forces in life such as the Worry Wartmonger and the Critical Wartmonger, you will END UP with baggage, whether you are aware you took it or not.

Baggage gets heavy and will slow you down. If you start acquiring too much baggage, you will become derailed.

You may feel like it's too much work to release or let go of your baggage (sometimes we think we deserve to carry certain burdens) *but it's more work to carry it.*

Remember these images when you think it's easier to carry emotional baggage: When someone worries you, you are carrying a fizzy drink with partially hydrogenated fingernails floating on top! When you accept criticism, you are carrying a smelly rotten fish with stingers and "Don't Worry Be Little" playing repetitively...

Travel Light

When you encounter negative forces along your path, usually it's an obstacle that you can and should turn into an opportunity to learn about yourself.

Always, always, always, there is a lesson hiding in every negative experience and you can CHOOSE to see your obstacle as a bad experience or you can CHOOSE to upgrade to the higher channel of thinking and see your obstacle as an opportunity to learn something new (about yourself, someone else or the world).

You are NOT meant to hold onto these experiences as baggage that will hold you back and keep you from reaching new heights. If you are holding on to self statements that are negative, such as anything you are NOT, those are FALSE creations of your ego mind or were implanted by someone else in your past or represent a person you are NO longer.

Release these ideas by imagining them as baggage you actually have to carry. If it's a memory, assign it a weight. Is it a 5 lb. memory or a 500 lb. memory? Assign your baggage a value because you ARE carrying it and it will weigh on you by turning into a bad habit, a dream never realized, or actual weight on your body.

You are meant to TRAVEL LIGHT. You are meant to keep on going, and no one can force you to hold on to that baggage EXCEPT YOU. You are the train. You decide your passengers who come along on your journey. You decide the cargo you carry.

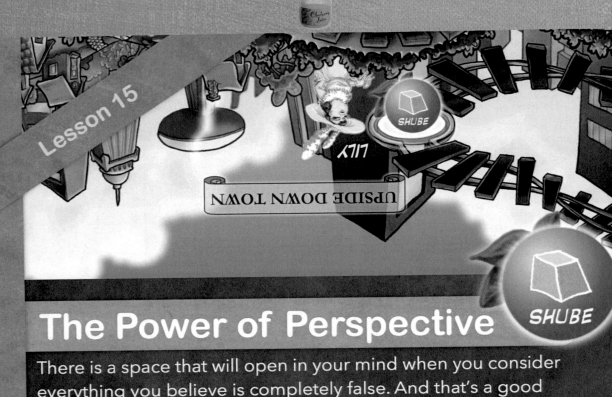

The Power of Perspective

There is a space that will open in your mind when you consider everything you believe is completely false. And that's a good space to have.

Consider all your beliefs about who you are and who other people are, what life means and why you are here living it. You may have a whole set of beliefs you are not even aware you hold and live out. Now, turn your beliefs upside down.

You may believe your life is meaningless: the exact opposite is true. Your life is meaningful beyond measure.

You may believe some people are more special than others: the exact opposite is true. We are ALL equally special.

There is great power in turning your beliefs upside down. Take any one belief you hold and spend a few moments believing the exact opposite. Just try it and watch how it creates space in your mind. The space invites new, refreshing perspectives to enter your mind.

Perspective is the power of the Shube Clueberry.

The Doubt Dragon

Being in a state of doubt is like entering a mini house filled with Staircases to Nowhere. You know you are IN DOUBT when you are questioning yourself. Questioning yourself is like looking in the mirror and actually saying, "I don't trust myself." Would you say that in the mirror? Probably not. In your mind, the act of doubting yourself leads to a series of useless thought process' much like walking up a series of Staircases to Nowhere (check out that map)!

So, how do you get out?

First recognize the Doubt Dragon has shown up and is whispering in your ear reasons to doubt yourself. You know you must be really getting somewhere because he only shows up when he sees someone steamrolling down their empowered path!

Receive the Doubt Dragon as a sign you're on track but DON'T let him get to you! Being too doubtful is how you get derailed.

What do you do about doubt? Don't trust it! The Doubt Dragon will try and make you doubtful of yourself. You know he has succeeded if you feel a fog of question marks radiating around you, causing confusion. To clear the fog of uncertainty, drop the baggage! The Doubt Dragon can't stand CERTAINTY. If your inner Doubt Dragon or someone else's Doubt Dragon is up in your face, respond with CERTAINTY.

This is called using affirmations and IT WORKS. Say sentences to yourself that start with I CAN or I AM.

You'll be moving away from him in less than 3 minutes and he'll be whimpering with his tail between his legs.

Here's a hint: you may not actually BELIEVE your CERTAINTY statement, but if you keep repeating it, you will be flooded with thoughts that lead to you believing it. So just do it.

Anyone who's achieved anything faces the Doubt Dragon. Everyone has to have their turn. Don't take it personally meaning don't doubt why you have doubt because that too will keep you stuck in a series of Staircases to Nowhere.

The Magic Toolshed

ZAR

Every single day of your life is surrounded with magic. So why doesn't life feel so magical? You are failing to SEE it. Your life is a gift to everyone around you. YOU are a gift to everyone you know. When you tap into this truth, you will begin to see magic everywhere...literally everywhere. Every pencil you hold has the magical capabilities to transform an idea in your mind into a project that could change your life, or a journal entry that will shift your entire understanding of your past or an idea on a note that you share that turns around someone else's life.

Where is magic? Everywhere you look. But the power of the Zar Clueberry is not about looking for magic; it's SEEING magic everywhere you look. There's magic in a staircase. There's magic in a mirror when you change what you say to yourself. There's magic in a door when you see it as a transition to another opportunity.

This is the amazing, awe inspiring thing about practicing the Zar Clueberry: magical experiences actually unfold in front of you when you see magic everywhere you look. The trick is this: *first YOU see it, and appreciate it and then MORE magic appears to you from every which direction.*

The Apathetic Alley Cats

Apathy is the opposite of passion. It's not caring. It is indifference. It is boredom to the max.

On the other hand, passion is an enthusiasm towards something that drives you or propels you to be excited about the journey of life. For some passion comes naturally. Others have to look for it.

Why care? Why become passionate? Passion is like a FUEL that gives you the best kind of energy: it eliminates the feeling of work from your life completely! You can be passionate about a sport, about creating art, about writing, about expressing yourself in theatre, about inspiring others, playing board games with friends, designing clothes, anything! You can even be passionate about another person like a great role model or author.

There are SO many things to be passionate about in life! If you make finding what gives you something to look forward to a priority early on in life, you will never feel like anything is a chore or work for you.

Map Check!
Where are we on the map?

3 Mindsets That'll Get You Lost in Life

My Way Mindset

You are heading in the wrong direction if you are not open to considering you made a mistake. Here are some signs: If you are following your own way and things aren't working, remember there are two channels our mind works on. Channel one WILL often lead you in the wrong direction. Stubbornness is a sign of your ego at work.

The This Way or That Way Mindset

You are heading in the wrong direction if you have this mindset. Here is a sign: you can't make a decision. Thinking about something is one thing but too much indecision leads you to confusion (stuck in the Maze with Godar, who you'll learn more about on the next page)!

The Follower Mindset

You are heading in the wrong direction if you are looking at someone else to lead you *for the wrong reasons*. Here's a scenario: your friend wants you to do something, try something or go somewhere that's not best for you and you follow anyway thinking it's hard to say no to a friend. This is taking a wrong turn and it's WAY harder to come back from a wrong turn than to stand your ground alone.

GODAR

ZECTANGLE

You come with a Clarity Compass

Lost? Confused? Go inward. Always.

The same MOMENT you forget to pay attention to your own thinking, your mind WILL default or flip back to Channel 1, the 24 hour of reruns of mostly negative thoughts and images. It's very easy to find yourself going along thinking your are on track and still end up in the Lazy Maze because we all tend to "fall sleep" or sleepwalk through certain parts of our day or situations.

Use Your Attention Anchor to anchor yourself in self-awareness. Look at your Think Tank. Is it murky and cluttered with shadowy thoughts? If so, just relax. That's the only way to let them settle and let the The Mircle (miracle thoughts) emerge. You really cannot perform a more important action that paying attention to your thoughts. Just don't add MORE clutter to the Think Tank by judging your thoughts. If you find yourself judging, focus on breathing in and out, in and out.

Clarity comes in the form of an illuminated thought. You will know clarity has set in your mind when you FEEL BETTER. Your FEELING GOOD is an indicator that your Clarity Compass is pointing you back in the right direction.

Clarity is the power of the Zectangle Clueberry.

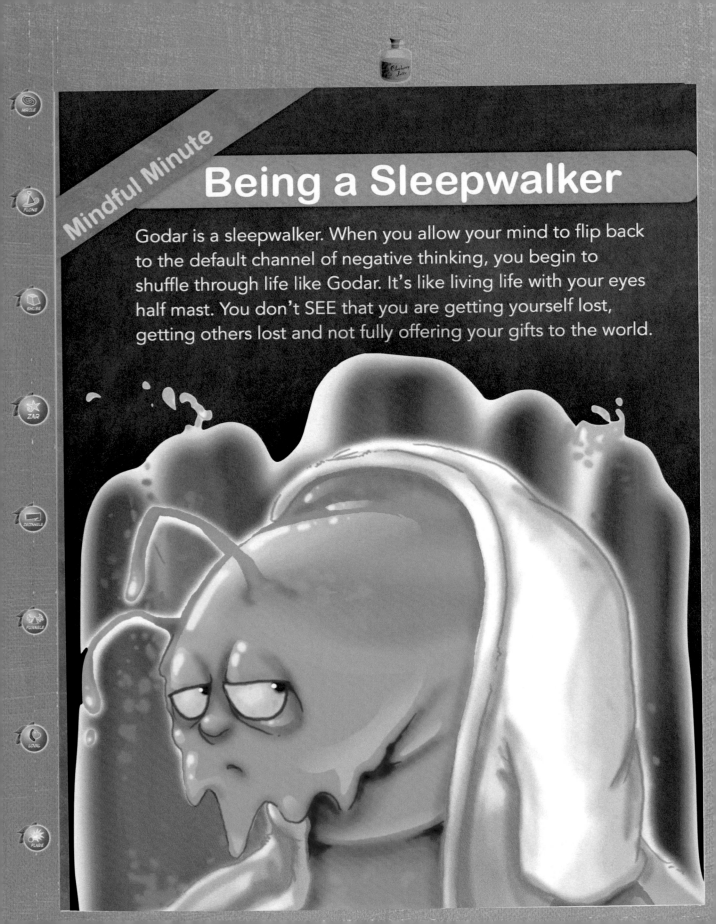

Being a Sleepwalker

Godar is a sleepwalker. When you allow your mind to flip back to the default channel of negative thinking, you begin to shuffle through life like Godar. It's like living life with your eyes half mast. You don't SEE that you are getting yourself lost, getting others lost and not fully offering your gifts to the world.

JUNGAR

FLIANGLE

OHM OCEAN

Be Like the Ocean

The constant circumstances of life that are disturbing, bothersome, uncomfortable and irritating are nothing more than the waves on the top of the ocean.

Life on the surface is just like the ocean's surface. Sometimes it is choppy and stormy and sometimes the surface of the ocean is calm. Deep down the ocean is undisturbed by whatever is going on the surface. You can be this way, too.

Life brings new experiences into life as new experiences end...just as the ocean ebbs and flows with the tide. Ohm Ocean represents the state of being that will help you stay on track. If you react to every little thing, you create MORE drama, waves, choppiness to experience.

Some experiences make you feel like you got splashed with cold water, other experiences like a giant wave crashed over your head, other experiences will feel like you are drowning way out in the dark ocean and no one is going to rescue you.

Every experience passes. The tide ebbs and flows, washing away the old and bringing the new. You can count on that!

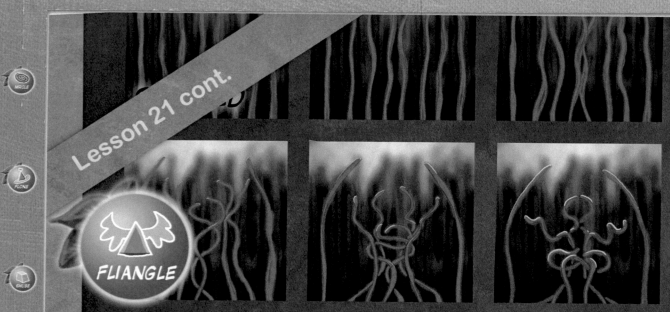

FLIANGLE

When the storm does pass, you may feel a little beat up by life, but deep down, like the ocean, there is a part of you that no one and nothing can hurt, damage or destroy.

In YOU there is an unimaginably deep still space made of a substance that seems to expand and become stronger with every experience you make it through.

When you're IN the storm, it's hard to believe the uncomfortable experience of being caught up in a storm (which usually in life is the experience of something being taken away from you) is actually for the purpose of ADDING to you in some way. Whatever it is that is being taken from you is expanding your soul tenfold. And that's something you actually can take with you when you die.

Allow yourself to be open to receiving signs. Signs emerge and show that within the seemingly messy chaos of life, there is order and harmony. If you align your nature with nature, signs will emerge and reveal themselves. To do this, trust that within all things, no matter how stormy, there is an order at work for the greatest good of all even if we don't understand, at first.

The power of the Fliangle Clueberry is intuition.

GUILT GHOST

There's nothing to be ashamed of.

Shame is a feeling that comes from guilt or embarrassment. It is a taunting emotion. Shame *emerges like an illusive phantom to taunt you like a ghost.* Shame causes you to get stuck in the Guilt Graveyard. Don't. Choose to work through it. This is how you know you are feeling shame:

1. Someone has intentionally or by accident, embarrassed or hurt you and you can't seem to put it behind you. You may either blame yourself or are confused as to your own role in what happened. The Guilt Ghost always sweeps in when you are confused about whether or not to take blame about a situation. Guilt sets in when you are wondering if you may have reacted wrong, or if something is all your fault, or when something happens that is not your fault one bit, even when you are baffled as to how it all unfolded like it did. The Guilt Ghost challenges you to examine WHICH, IF ANY part you take responsibility for, claim that part, make amends, forgive yourself and move on. Sometimes, because of what someone else did, or because you are trying to work through your own responsibility, you feel stuck, perhaps because you feel flawed, damaged or different. It may take time to get past the Guilt Graveyard. Just know nothing you did or someone else did can damage you, only cause you grow.

2. Another form of shame and embarrassment is humiliation. Humiliation happens in public and is caused by someone else trying to squash you and make you feel small in front of others so that they can appear big and important or so they can deflect attention away from their own insecurities by attempting to put the spotlight on you. The Guilt Ghost likes to remind you of past humiliating moments each time you want to try something new. Suddenly, you'll find yourself feeling like you cannot do something or your are overcome with fear because the Guilt Ghost is taunting you with some memory trying to holding you back. As painful as it can be, you can defeat the Guilt Ghost if you do the exact thing that scares you because you are facing the fear of humiliation again, and when you face that fear, you have defeated it, regardless of the outcome. The Guilt Ghost likes to twist mistakes into your FAILURES as opposed to learning lessons. If you buy into that, you'll be cringing when you recall these experiences. Defeat the Guilt Ghost by redefining your mistakes as learning lessons.

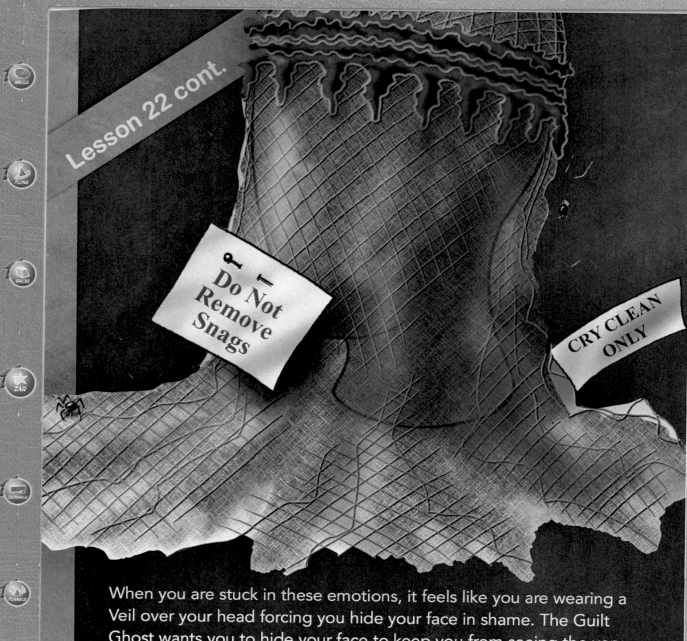

When you are stuck in these emotions, it feels like you are wearing a Veil over your head forcing you hide your face in shame. The Guilt Ghost wants you to hide your face to keep you from seeing the very bright future ahead of you! Being stuck in shame is being stuck in the Guilt Graveyard because it is its like trying to live a life and find happiness among dead things that haunt you. You are meant to evolve, to begin anew, to release the past. Chances are very strong, whatever caused the shame was not your fault and the way out is to ACCEPT that you are FREE to move on. There are tracks in front of the Guilt Graveyard. Don't get tricked into being stuck wallowing in your past. Get back on track. Keep on going. Leave your past behind you. See what's in store for you up ahead!

Refuse the Bitter Beets.

It's normal and healthy to feel anger. We all have an Angry Android inside us. Anger is a strong emotion with lots of energy behind. There can be a benefit to anger. If channeled positively, it can turn into passion.

On the other hand, when you hold on to anger or it sits IN you, that's called stewing. If anger isn't burned off in the form of healthy action, it WILL turn into bitterness. Actually it turns YOU bitter.

When the Angry Android rises up in you, the absolute fastest way to cool down its temps is to get air. You don't have to go outside or take a walk, even. Simply inhale for 5 seconds, hold it for 5 seconds and exhale for 5 seconds. Repeat. It's so simple but it works. When you get heated, and don't halt the rising temps, you'll get burned, eventually, and in the very least be stuck having the taste of Bitter Beets in your mouth all the time!

MR. QUO

The Status Quo will drain you.

The Status Quo means as things are.

Let go of trying to fit in with things as they are. It will always drain you. If you are uncomfortable and frustrated with where you are, with the way things are, it means you are ready to take a leap of faith into pursuing your passion, purpose, dreams and ambition.

Mr. Quo represents the experience of being DRAINED. If you feel drained you are in a place that isn't supporting the growth of your passion, purpose, ambition and dreams.

Use this experience to see what dream you'd like to pursue. Sometimes we figure out what we want by experiencing what we do not want.

PASSION

AMBITION

PURPOSE

DREAMS

There's lots of hogwash in the news.

By now, you have learned to pay attention and understand how important paying attention can be. What you pay attention to in life IS a true investment in the direction of your life.

There's lots to pay attention to in life. Beware of The Exaggeration Ox. He can be a HUGE source of fear if we pay attention to him. Since he writes a lot of the headlines and news stories in the world and since reporting the news is a really HUGE responsibility, you'd think what he says is TRUE.

A lot of the time it's exaggerated hogwash! The Ox has a BIG mouth and loves to create more drama to help sell his newspapers.

Don't get overly scared by the nature of the Ox delivering news.
Know the Exaggeration Ox's true motive is not to sell the truth: he has a product CALLED the newspaper to sell. And exaggeration sells.

So when paying attention to the newspaper, consider it may be hogwash.

TREEHOUSE

MALVIN
TAILFEATHER

LOVAL

Loving vs. Fearful Intention

Always remember this weak little creature named Tailfeather sitting in a rickety old tree house when you are letting your fear get the best of you. He's the Father of all Fear.

He, along with his wife Foggy, the Mother of Ignorance created ALL the little monsters that try and derail you in your life. All their little monsters like the Worry Wartmonger and the Doubt Dragon, are just blocks from YOU loving yourself and living out YOUR genius. They want to make you act, think and behave out of fear. Don't let this weak little phantom and his sinister dung beetle wife knock you off the track of your life or trap you in fear. Making an effort to choose loving actions towards yourself and others over fearful thoughts like worry, doubt, criticism, guilt and anger in every moment of every day is the power of the Loval Clueberry at work inside you. The paradox is that the meanest, nastiest, most selfish experiences come from those acting out of their own fear. When you know this, it makes it a little bit easier to forego responding with your fear to their fear. It's all about choosing a more empowering intention for your own life. It's not easy to choose love over fear, but try. Sometimes choosing love is standing up for the truth and others will make you feel like you're being negative. It can be confusing, at times. All you can all do is try.

You are not here to be perfect. You are here to learn.

Invisible Thresholds and Quantum Leaps

When you are ready to take a step out of mediocrity in your life, it may only seem like a small thing: a DECISION YOU MADE. However, when that decision is towards achieving your dreams or exercising your genius, you are taking a step that is actually a quantum leap crossing an Invisible Threshold.

That's because you are now crossing over the Chasm of Infinite Fear.

It's a wonderfully exciting experience because YOU have come so far! And you are choosing to look IN the face of your past guilts, your past doubts, your past worries and past criticisms and jump across ALL of it believing in something, having faith in the future, trusting the process, knowing deep inside the BEST IS YET TO COME IN YOUR LIFE!

You are now a Vision Seeker, "One who sees the way!"

FLARE

Clueberry Juice

The ability to see with insight

FLARE

When you can recognize fear forms in yourself and others, you have a greater ability to access your power of insight.

The power of insight is the final clueberry called the Flare Clueberry. It means "to see". This kind of seeing is not with your outer eyes but your inner eye. Insight is the power to access a deep truth and see reality from a big picture.

The Flare Clueberry is an aspect of your consciousness that is activated once all the other Clueberries are awakened in your consciousness.

Clueberry Review

SEEKER NOTES

1. MIRCLE = USEFUL IDEA
2. OBSERVE THE THINK TANK
3. USELESS MIRCLES CLUTTER THE SURFACE
4. PATIENCE !
5. USEFUL MIRCLES EMERGE
6. DON'T JUMP IN !
7. I CREATE MIRCLES BY THINKING

MIRCLE

SEEKER NOTES

1. ZECTANGLE = CLARITY
2. THREE CONFUSION MINDSETS
3. ONE WAY OUT - INWARD

ZECTANGLE

SEEKER NOTES

1. SHUBE = CONSIDER 6 SIDES
2. SIDES CAN BE PERSPECTIVES, IDEAS, OBJECTS

SHUBE

SEEKER NOTES

1. FLONE = ATTRACT WHAT YOU NEED FOR YOUR MIRCLE
2. KNOW WHAT YOU NEED
3. ATTRACT NOT SEARCH
4. WEAR MASK AT ALL TIMES
5. RECEIVE !

FLONE

SEEKER NOTES

1. FLIANGLE = MESSAGES FROM THE UNIVERSE
2. BE LIKE THE OCEAN
3. CHOPPY ON THE SURFACE, STILLNESS DEEP DOWN
4. SURRENDER TO EBB AND FLOW

FLIANGLE

SEEKER NOTES

1. ZAR = MAGIC IN EVERY DAY TOOLS
2. MUNDANE MAGIC

ZAR

SEEKER NOTES

1. LOVAL = LOVE OR FEAR IS AT THE ROOT OF EVERYTHING
2. FEAR MANIFESTS IN MANY FORMS

LOVAL

SEEKER NOTES

1. FLARE = TO SEE
2. INSIGHT
3. THIRD EYE TO SEE INVISIBLE THINGS

FLARE

CLUEBERRY WORLD TOUR

Clueberry World Tour

a journey to discover self respect

Edgar Dupin

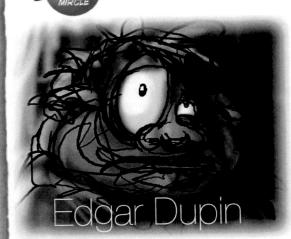

I'm Edgar Dupin, your tour guide today. As I take you through the different states on the map, remember this map is a map of your mind. That means the states represent states of mind. Here you'll gain the clues that'll lead to achieving your dreams and learn what stands in the way of your dreams.

In this world, there are eight clues to being on track with a positive train of thought everyday. In Clueberry World, they are called Clueberries.

The eight Clueberries are powers of your mind:

thought, possibility, perspective, creativity, clarity, attention, decision and insight.

These inner powers are what cultivate and nurture your self respect and self worth every single day. What you will learn is you already possess these powers of your mind and that it's what's sabotaging you every day is the REAL journey of Clueberry World. You'll learn how to to navigate through all the obstacles to all your dreams for the rest of your life!

"Expect eight stops along the way where you will meet your Clueberry teachers. There will also be encounters with creatures who will do their best to sabotage your success! It all starts at the Think Tank, where I teach you the first lesson about your mind. I'll tell you how the Think Tank works in a minute but first, meet your saboteurs.

Tailfeather

These creatures or saboteurs are the children of Malvin Tailfeather, the "father of fear." Their main mission is to derail you on your path towards achieving your dreams.

Greed Fiend

I will show you how to respond to the saboteurs as they work to fill your head with negative thoughts. However, after this tour, it's up to YOU to defeat all twelve saboteurs all on your own...every day.
Below are these are the faces of all the awkward creatures you'll encounter along the tracks and on the next page, you'll meet all your teachers.

Find them on the map!

Worry Wartmonger   Guilt Ghost   Critical Wartmonger   Insincerity Ogre   Angry Android

Apathetic Alley Cats   Doubt Dragon   Anxiety Android   Mr. and Mrs. Bully   Mr. Quo

SABOTEURS

CLUEBERRY TEACHERS:

 EDGAR
THE THINK TANK
 MIRCLE → power of thought

 **CROCKER**
THE JUNKYARD
 FLONE → power of possibility

 **LILY**
UPSIDE DOWN TOWN
 SHUBE → power of perspective

 **DEXTER**
THE MAGIC TOOLSHED
 ZAR → power of creativity

 **GODAR**
LAZY MAZE
 ZECTANGLE → power of clarity

 **JUNGAR**
OHM OCEAN
 FLIANGLE → power of attention

 **TAILFEATHER**
THE TREEHOUSE
 LOVAL → power of decision

 GROOGLES
THE VISION MACHINE
FLARE → power of insight

Think Tank

Train of Thought

MR. & MRS BULLY

TOOL

Power of thought

MIRCLE

Clueberry World is a school with different kind of lessons. It's a SCHOOL OF THOUGHT. When you look at the map of Clueberry World, you will see that there are states like any other map, but the states represent states of MIND. Each place on the map has a teacher who guides you to becoming more aware of how your mind works.

Before I introduce the first lesson, let's address the core question you will inevitably ask: WHY? All my students always ask me that! They'd say, "Why are we doing this? Why do I have to learn this? Will I use this in real life?" It's a great question! When we know WHY, we are highly motivated to learn, and engage all our efforts and focus. So, I'll tell you WHY you are in Clueberry World, the School of Thought.

Thoughts are like seeds that stem into beliefs which blossom into decisions that create the nature of your life.

Clueberry World clues you into your inner world because while there are some constants or fixed elements that make up the nature of your life such as the race or heritage you belong to, or the part of the world you come from, how you think is always in your control. Because life comes with individual struggles and challenges that direct and shape your path in the world, the work in Clueberry World is about learning how to interpret life's obstacles and struggles in a way that is empowering. Your awareness of your train of thought has the power to keep you on track or derailed as you travel through life.

Take a closer look at the Think Tank, where you'll learn about your first Clueberry called the Mircle, the power of a THOUGHT. Thoughts are negative and positive. How do you know the difference? By how a thought makes you FEEL. Positive thoughts bring about **feelings of calm, a sense of excitement, hope, joy, inspiration, enthusiasm, understanding** and more. Negative thoughts bring about feelings of fear such as doubt, anxiety, anger, confusion, and more. Positive thoughts expand into motivation and lead to action and decision. Negative thoughts cause you to shrink and lead to inaction and fear. We will learn how negative thoughts work from the saboteur creatures stationed around the Clueberry map. The more you practice facing them and getting to know them personally, the less they can derail you!

The Mircle is all about becoming AWARE of your thoughts. Becoming aware of your thoughts is how you begin to take control over your train of thought as being derailed or on track.

THE JUNKYARD

FLONE

CROCKER

"Find the Junkyard on the map and let's meet Crocker. Don't judge Crocker on his looks, or the fact that he loves junk. More than that, he BELIEVES in junk because he knows every Mircle idea can be turned into its physical equivalent if you have what you need to make it. And that's where believing in junk comes in! Most of the time, we don't have what we need for our dreams and vision to manifest. While others may see themselves surrounded by junk, Crocker sees potential. Let's introduce you. Hey Crocker! Look here. We got a whole train full of untapped talent!"

"Hey, kids, lemme show you how the Flone works while you're here. Just going over it real quick. There's a lot more to it than this but here's a quickie version. All you have to do is put on my Magnet Mask. You speak into it, loud and clear, what you need for your Mircle idea.

All you have to say is, "everything I need is coming to me right now." Say it loud! You can also say, "I am attracting everything I need right now!" Then, watch out. Sometimes, you'll be surprised by what you attract. In no time, all kinds of stuff from every direction will rise up out of the Junkyard and come whizzing through the air at you!

To activate this power inside you, will require you to have belief in the possibilities that lie under the surface...there's always possibilities under the surface..always. You don't have to know what they are, just that they ARE there waiting for you to discover them."

TOOL

PARENTS & EDUCATORS: Ask kids to consider times when something appeared hopeless, a big mess or overwhelming but turned out to have an unexpectedly great outcome. What does the statment: "letting go of junk uncovers possibilities" mean to you?

Oh, there's Oggie and Mo. They aren't exactly considered sabotuers in Clueberry World but they sometimes act like it! You'll see. Everybody sit up a little straighter. They are the Rulers of the World. It doesn't mean what you think. Remember this whole world is about changing how you think. Rulers just make up rules. That's about their only purpose in the world. Oggie is the King of Empty Catchphrases and Mo is the Queen of Lip Service. Hi Oggie and Mo! Would you mind just a few Empty Catchphrases or some Lip Service for our new kids?

Find Oggie and Mo on the map:

Oh, um, er, greetings Edgar. What do we have here? Oh, it's the newbies. Well, on behalf of the World Council, let me extend my warmest welcomes to all of you. Good luck on your journey. This is where you can find us. We really never go anywhere, since we spend a lot of time signing and stamping and holding meetings to determine when other meetings will be held, and well, we do welcome feedback. However, we never respond to complaints. They are swept under the World Council rug. Anyway, uh, Mo? A few words?

Maybe next time... I am actually busy enjoying this sandwich. I do however need to clarify one point. Be advised that the World Council closes from 1-6 pm for lunch hours, regardless of how serious or pressing the matter. I suggest Seekers write 5 consecutive letters to make an appointment and we will respond with a meeting date within 8-12 months. We always take every world matter seriously. As I always say, over and over and over, "We will review this matter very seriously and certainly look into it."

PARENTS & EDUCATORS: Ask kids to think of a time rules and laws seemed to keep them from moving forward. Come up with a few examples of bureaucracy.

Great Mo. Well, enjoy your sandwich! Thanks, see you soon, I am sure! We'll be on our way now... Okay, now that we're out of earshot I have to tell you not to trust those two, okay? Don't expect they have your best interest or the interest of the world at heart. They have a real important job, but unfortunately they love the power of sitting up higher than the rest of us in those fancy red velvet council chairs more than they care about solving world problems. Oh jeepers, here we go! Brace yourself! Writer's Block is upon is!

Find Writer's Block on the Clueberry map:

WORRY WARTMONGER

UGLY WARTMONGER

CRITICAL WARTMONGER

Well look who it is! An entire train of new kids! I'd say good luck but I don't see any potential in any of you. You all look like a bunch of nobodies. I can you tell how you're dressed. Well, it looks like I have gotten to some of you! Can't think of anything to say? Come over here, take some of my D Grade Carp for your backpack.

D Grade Carp

100% D Grade Carp

"Don't Worry Be Little"

Alright everybody, quick. Act confident! She's trying to degrade you and The Critical Wartmonger doesn't like confidence at all. Point out something perfect about yourself. It could be anything! Do it now! Okay, let's see if it worked. Yup, there she goes, back into her apartment. You don't want her baggage - defeating her is a good thing. It's a big smelly rotten fish, and it has scorpion-like stingers that seem to have a life of their own. Would you want to carry something like that in your backpack? Be confident around her and you won't have to. Uh oh. Here we go again! There's the Ugly Wartmonger.

PARENTS & EDUCATORS: Ask kids: What is criticism? Who has criticized you and how did it make you feel? Did you find yourself believing that person and taking on their criticism? Has criticism become an obstacle in your ability to feel great about who you are?

Hey. I say HEY. Look at me when I'm talking to you. What do you think you're doing here? Who you think you are? I'll tell you. Just a bunch of newbies and you're NO match for me. Watch out. I'll block you every time you try and make a change in this world or in yourself. I hate change. I revolt against it. And that includes update, revising, re-thinking, and that also includes even considering updating, revising or rethinking. I don't understand why change is necessary and I am here to make sure I do all I can to get in your way. I'll be after each and every one of you... and I don't forget a face. I hope you don't forget mine. Pitiful group of hopefuls is all you are.

Everybody, quick, before he gets to you too much, do something silly. Do a funky dance, wiggle your hips and wave your arms around. The Ugly Wartmonger doesn't like silliness or lightness at all because he might crack a smile and take life less seriously. A smile would probably make him less ugly, too and that's not what he wants. He'd rather be ugly.

His job is basically to spew off ignorance, ignorance and more ignorance. He is highly negative, full of "can'ts" and hates and no's and huffs and puffs and well, in short, he's all around got a really closed up mind.

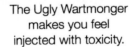

Hanging around him too long feels like you got a shot of 100% pure toxins straight into your blood stream. Oh it's just awful. If you can get your hands on some wisdom like a good book, that's the kind of brain powder that can help you reverse the effects of ignorance.

The Ugly Wartmonger makes you feel injected with toxicity.

Get ready...we are about to encounter the Worry Wartmonger!

PARENTS & EDUCATORS: Ask kids: What does ignorance mean exactly? How does ignorance present itself within you? What are you ignorant about? Edgar explains it means a "closed mind" but it can also mean lack of knowledge. Do you know anyone who you'd describe as ignorant? How has ignorance hurt people in the past? How has ignorance hurt you? How can ignorance keep you from feeling respect for yourself and feeling great about who you are as a person?

"Oh geez. More kids. All I have to say is don't forget to ask all the things that could go wrong. They never tell you about all the stuff you should be worrying about. That's why I am here, to remind you to worry. I have a couple cans of Vex I just opened with fresh brouhaha, artificial hubbub syrup, partially hydrogenated fingernails (I just bit them off this morning!) floating on top, especially for you!"

Gross! That stuff will really upset your stomach. Just give her a big wave and a smile. She wants to see you frowning, furrowing your eyebrows in concern, and biting your fingernails. She's always biting her fingernails!

PARENTS & EDUCATORS: Ask kids what worries them. Has there ever been a situation they were worried about that turned out to be no big deal?

DRONE GIANT

Next stop is Coffee & Dronuts! The Drone Giant seems like a pretty harmless monster but he spends his whole day droning to anyone who'll listen. Good thing he's not around right now. He can hold us up from moving forward and LOVES to waste time. If you fall for his long winded ramblings about what he'd do if he was in charge and his plans for the future and stories from his past, then you are becoming idle...and have to hold onto an ACTUAL Idler...which really weighs you down!

Who wants to carry around a rusty, old piece of an engine that says, 'Out of Operation?! It was made by Useless Endeavors, a division of Dronuts...

Made by USELESS ENDEAVORS
A Division of Dronuts

Out of Operation Since

PARENTS & EDUCATORS: Ask kids what it means to "waste time", procrastinate, or put something off. What causes procrastination? What internal blocks keeps us from just doing something?

UPSIDE DOWN TOWN

LILY

SHUBE

Here we go! Now off to Upside Down Town! I know none of you are used to hanging upside down. The reason this state is important is because you see things from perspectives you never thought of before and here you will learn how to the see the world in a new way! It's pretty cool indeed. Perspective is the power to consider many different viewpoints.

If you can see things through other people's perspectives, it radically changes how you make decisions! By the way, this is not just about seeing things from other people's perspectives, it's also seeing things from the perspective of a place, or how one idea effects another.

Lily is the Mayor's wife in Upside Down Town as well as the Shube Clueberry teacher. She's a bit of a diva, but she has to be. The Mayor of this town is her husband and she spends most of her time doing his job. Don't tell either of them I said that. There she is now! Hey Lily, we got a train full of untapped talent here ready to learn about the Shube Clueberry!"

MAYOR

Darlings...hello. I'll make this quick. I know being upside down can be uncomfortable the first couple of times. The Shube Clueberry is all about gaining different perspectives about ideas and people and places. We like to suggest exercising your mind by considering 6 different perspectives for everything. It seems like a lot, doesn't it? It's how you begin to gain perspective and quite honestly, perspective helps prevent problems because you are thinking THROUGH something really thoroughly. Until you get the hang of thinking about 6 different sides to any one idea, you can use my Shube Globe. Just press of a button to hear different perspectives from all over the world. I see a whole lot of upside down faces looking pretty red and uncomfortable, so carry on!

SHUBE

THE POWER TO GAIN PERSPECTIVE

EDUCATOR & PARENTS: Ask children to think of a situation that many people cannot agree on. Ask them to see the different sides of each person's perspective to the situation. It could be a big world issue like war, a local issue or family situation.

Well look who it is, a train full of new talent. Don't you doubt that you have talent? I do. I mean really. Has anyone ever called you new talent before? Didn't think so. Edgar's just trying to give you a false sense of confidence. Maybe you have *no* talent. Here, take this special coin I call a Qualm. It'll help clear things up.

Enough already Doubt Dragon. The only thing that Qualm does is radiate a fog of question marks! You're coming on a bit thick today, aren't you? *As you know*, these kids wouldn't be here if they weren't untapped talent. *As you well know*, every child possesses untapped potential. *As you very well know*, it only takes learning Clueberry powers for each child to tap into their talents. Now shrink away, or at least get out of our way.

Doubt works in the early stages of dream vision seeking, Edger...I am proud to have derailed millions of kids by causing just a teeny weeny bit of self doubt in them. I am sure I will see you all very soon...Say hi to Dexter for me!

PARENTS & EDUCATORS: Ask children to describe when they felt doubtful. How can self-doubt be overcome when we feel overwhelmed with confusion? What if someone else doubts us? Does someone else's doubt become our own doubt?

ZAR

Welcome to the Magic Toolshed! Here I teach you the power of the Zar Clueberry. Zar is the power of your creativity. Here's just one example of what I teach you: how to see everyday tools as having the power to change your life. Take a pencil, for example. When you use it to write statements that begin with "I am_____" it becomes pure magic. I teach you how to work with what you have by SEEING tools are all around you. There's another example on the next page called the Frame of Mind. An ordinary picture frame has the power to frame circumstances, events, ideas, encounters. This means you can frame things however you CHOOSE to. When you apply this power to circumstances that are negative, you can change them to positive or see a lesson emerge. So, applying the creative power of your mind (called the zar clueberry) to a boring old picture frame, instantly changes how you frame things. That means, what you see and focus on also changes in an instant, too.

Lesson 1:
THE FRAME OF MIND

PARENTS & EDUCATORS: Ask kids to think about a situation that could change if they saw it differently. Ask kids to look around and find every day objects that have a purpose that is much more important they initially realized.

Thanks Dexter, for that important lesson. My favorite lesson is called "The Mundane Magic Wand: how to change your life with a pencil." We're so conditioned to thinking pencils are for filling in bubbles, we forget that they can transform ideas into visions that may change the world! Writing down your thoughts, outlining your ideas, or jotting down positive statements creates an "unwritten" contract with deepest inner self. Right now, go find a regular old pencil.

This is the part that may not seem that powerful to you, but it is: first, write down an idea that will make the world a better place. Second, write down one positive statement about yourself that begins I AM. Third, write down one sentence that describes who you want to BE in 5 years. Really do this. We are about to encounter the Apathetic Alley Cats so it's best to get down a few great thoughts and before they tell you how lazy you could be in life."

PARENTS & EDUCATORS: Help children think of ideas that make the world better by thinking about their local community, their own school or what would improve their own life. It doesn't have to be a HUGE change. Minor changes often make the biggest difference. Encourage kids to see how writing down ideas bring about small inner shifts that cause major boosts in positive energy.

Excuse us while we yaaaawwwwwwn. Okay, much better. Come over here you newbies. So this is what we do all day. You're looking at it. We love to sit around all day. Sometimes, we groom ourselves. That's one of our favorite Pass Times. We just love passing time. We have a welcoming present for you too. It's a ticket to our favorite seats: on the fence. Excuse us while we get back to another Pass Time, napping....Yaaaawwwwwnnnnnnn. Come back later after our nap...I'm sure you'll find yourself lost in the Maze any minute...since....Godar....isZZZZZZZZZZ....

PARENTS & EDUCATORS: Ask kids the difference between relaxing and laziness and disinterest. Ask children to describe when they are lazy and when they relax and when they simply just don't care at all. Think of examples of where you'd like to be inspired but don't care it all. What would it take to be inspired about something when you don't care about it at all?

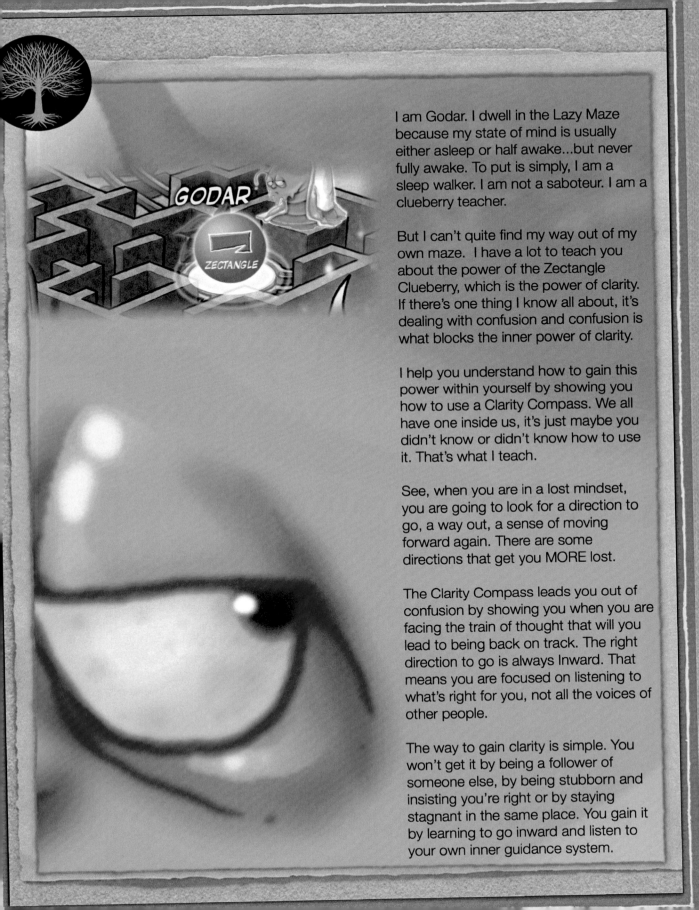

I am Godar. I dwell in the Lazy Maze because my state of mind is usually either asleep or half awake...but never fully awake. To put is simply, I am a sleep walker. I am not a saboteur. I am a clueberry teacher.

But I can't quite find my way out of my own maze. I have a lot to teach you about the power of the Zectangle Clueberry, which is the power of clarity. If there's one thing I know all about, it's dealing with confusion and confusion is what blocks the inner power of clarity.

I help you understand how to gain this power within yourself by showing you how to use a Clarity Compass. We all have one inside us, it's just maybe you didn't know or didn't know how to use it. That's what I teach.

See, when you are in a lost mindset, you are going to look for a direction to go, a way out, a sense of moving forward again. There are some directions that get you MORE lost.

The Clarity Compass leads you out of confusion by showing you when you are facing the train of thought that will you lead to being back on track. The right direction to go is always Inward. That means you are focused on listening to what's right for you, not all the voices of other people.

The way to gain clarity is simple. You won't get it by being a follower of someone else, by being stubborn and insisting you're right or by staying stagnant in the same place. You gain it by learning to go inward and listen to your own inner guidance system.

Godar, I think that's the longest you've ever stayed awake and remained clear enough to talk about clarity in a clear way. Your eyes always glaze over and you sink into....oh wait, Godar? Godar? Ok, well we lost him. That's what happens. Let's all take a copy of his lesson notes because we will all eventually get lost and confused, and typically when you are lost and confused, you are also lost and confused about who told you what to do when you are lost and confused...Or something like that. Let's grab those notes.

HOW TO GAIN CLARITY

If you are reading this, I am unavailable. So here's the big lesson I learned about how to get clear.

FIRST, what will get you even more lost are 3 mindsets. I drew pictures of them on the chalkboards.

To find your way out of the maze, don't look outside of yourself, go inward. You have an inner compass to guide you that only works for you when you stop looking in the wrong direction which is by looking outside yourself.

Let's go check out the chalk boards. On a side note, being a sleepwalker means you're unreliable! One minute you're available, the next you're not. You don't ever want to get stuck in the Maze mindset for long and end up like Godar. Godar is a great clueberry teacher because he means no harm to anyone. He doesn't try to sabotage you on purpose like the other saboteurs. However, sleepwalkers are very frustrating to deal with. They are only partially engaged with life and this means they really only lose out, however if you encounter one, be careful not to depend too heavily on them. Okay, onward to the read the chalk boards he left us.

THE 3 MINDSETS TO AVOID WHEN YOU'RE TRYING TO TAP INTO YOUR INNER CLARITY COMPASS

WISHWASHY MINDSET

the fear of making the wrong decision will keep you from taking a first step at all

STUBBORN MINDSET

the <u>un</u>willingness to see a different way than your own way will keep you at a standstill

FOLLOWER MINDSET

to avoid mustering the courage to trust your own instincts or be a leader, it will appear an easier route to let someone else lead even if their way
is not best for you

INWARD

confusion is uncomfortable causing you to want "do something about it" however if you are still for a moment and <u>allow yourself to feel the discomfort</u>, it will begin to vanish naturally revealing your inner clarity compass, which will then <u>point to</u> or <u>make clear</u> the direction you need to take

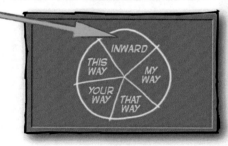

Basically, it looks like Godar is saying that it's important to never get stuck in your own ways, follow someone else's way, or to wander around without direction. Clear your mind, relax, and you'll find your own inner compass. The Zectangle Clueberry is about learning to naturally end up out of the confusion of the maze. OH NO! Look who we have here. The Bullies are brutal. Here we go. Just let me take care of them since this is your first time meeting them in Clueberry World.

Well, well, well, look who we have here. If it isn't a train full of new talent. Move over. We're getting on the train to get a good hard look at your bunch of losers. Look at her! Look at him! Hahaha! Nice outfit. Nice face! Hahaha. Not. All we see are a bunch of losers who should be sent back where they came from. None of you belong here, not one of you. Let's spit on them!

Spitting? Insulting kids for their clothes? I wouldn't expect anything less from you, Mr. and Mrs. Bully. Do you feel special now? Who exactly are you talking to? It couldn't be us. Go find something else to do. It's pathetic that harassing kids entertains you. Get a life! Bye now. Sorry your efforts didn't work out for you today.

PARENTS & EDUCATORS: Ask kids if they have ever been bullied, bullied someone else or witnessed someone being bullied. What motivates a bully? Is bullying the same as harassment? What happens to a person inside when he/she is bullied?

They are so....awful. I really dislike the bullies. Oh, my goodness, not again! It's another monster. This guy's called the Insincerity Ogre. He's not as outright mean as the Bullies.

Oh lovely! Delightful! Fabulous! I am always delighted and overjoyed to meet new talent. Oh, I can see some real potential here in these kids. You have a glimmer, you are going to be great, you have a real way with words, you are going be a singer, you look like a dancer...."

Thank you for all those sincerely nice things you said Insincerity Ogre. We really do have to get along now.

Oh stay. I want to hear all about the new talent. I want to hear about their ideas, and I want to support their ideas and give 'em a good old pat on the head, a really sincere *'good luck with that'* or a *'I believe in you'* and that's just the kind of guy I am. I am here to listen with a passive ear and actively share my insincere hopes for all your success.

Bye Insincerity Ogre! Go eat some of that fake ham you're always trying to feed everyone! His whole job is to inflate you with false support to distract and derail you. He means nothing he says. Most unauthentic person you'll ever meet. Up next, we find the Anxiety Android.

Yikes, oh no, I am a wreck right now. I can't talk to anyone I know, never mind meeting a bunch of kids I don't know! Get them away from me. I am a basket case. In fact, do any of you want to share in being a basket case with me? I would feel so much less anxious if I could make you anxious, too...

Thanks for the offer but we are just doing a quick tour of Clueberry World! Not many people enjoy getting turned into a basket case, Anxiety Android. I know how much you'd like us to join you in your basket case but we are going to skip along to Mr. Quo...Okay kids, so let me give you a recap of what's going on...

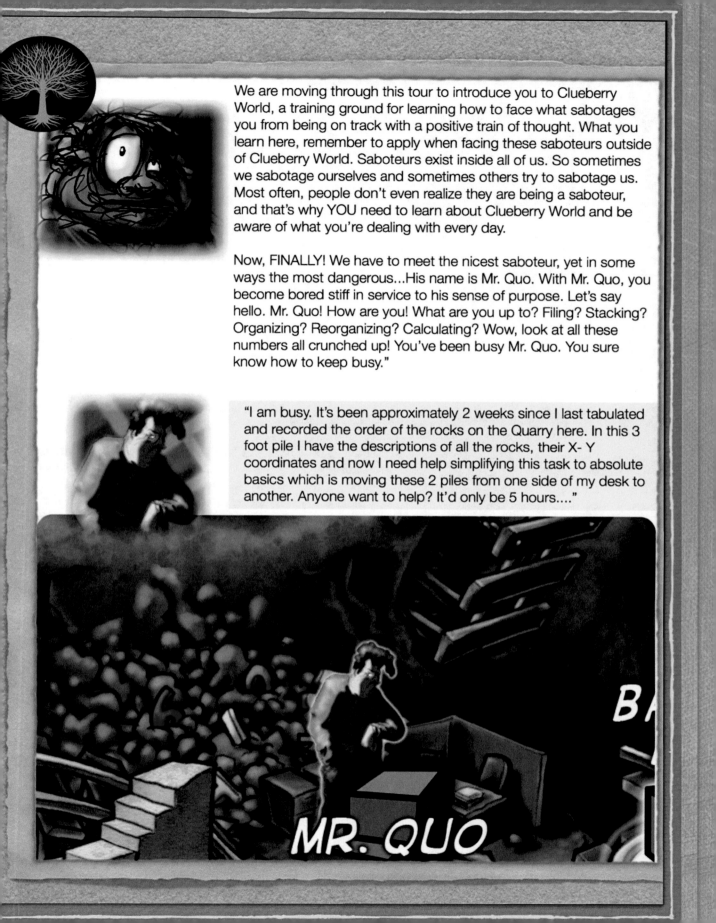

We are moving through this tour to introduce you to Clueberry World, a training ground for learning how to face what sabotages you from being on track with a positive train of thought. What you learn here, remember to apply when facing these saboteurs outside of Clueberry World. Saboteurs exist inside all of us. So sometimes we sabotage ourselves and sometimes others try to sabotage us. Most often, people don't even realize they are being a saboteur, and that's why YOU need to learn about Clueberry World and be aware of what you're dealing with every day.

Now, FINALLY! We have to meet the nicest saboteur, yet in some ways the most dangerous...His name is Mr. Quo. With Mr. Quo, you become bored stiff in service to his sense of purpose. Let's say hello. Mr. Quo! How are you! What are you up to? Filing? Stacking? Organizing? Reorganizing? Calculating? Wow, look at all these numbers all crunched up! You've been busy Mr. Quo. You sure know how to keep busy."

"I am busy. It's been approximately 2 weeks since I last tabulated and recorded the order of the rocks on the Quarry here. In this 3 foot pile I have the descriptions of all the rocks, their X- Y coordinates and now I need help simplifying this task to absolute basics which is moving these 2 piles from one side of my desk to another. Anyone want to help? It'd only be 5 hours...."

B

MR. QUO

Thanks Mr. Quo. That sounds riveting. We are on a quick and brief tour to introduce all the kids to Clueberry World. I am sure when they return you will be doing something similar and they will have the opportunity to experience your busy work.

So, we are reaching the final destination in our tour: The Vision Machine. It's where you learn the final clueberry power.

Welcome to the Vision Machine! I'm Professor Groogles! Here you learn about your ability to see the world and yourself through a lens without fear. It's the power of the Flare Clueberry and it means to see.

Clueberry World teaches you that you ARE capable of seeing who you are without the distorted thoughts of your inner Critical Wartmonger and inner Doubt Dragon in your ear, to see the beauty of your circumstances as containing lessons that teach you to develop self confidence, and to see your relationships through the lens of a bigger picture.

The Flare Clueberry is the final ingredient in an exilir that we call Clueberry Juice. It's your inner potion created by all the Clueberry powers when you are fully empowered to slay saboteurs every day and you can access your inner clueberry powers at any time no matter what. This potion depletes and re-fills according to your doing the great work of traveling your own mind map defeating your inner and outer saboteurs, and expanding your mind in the process.

The process of putting to action a daily practice of being self aware, of being aware of your encounters, when you're derailed and off track will build your self respect, self confidence and self esteem. This is the way to achievement in all areas of your life. It is also the way to cope, process, shift your mood and overcome obstacles.

Clueberry Juice is like your personal container measuring your level of staying true to YOUR truth, to your level of commitment in developing who YOU are supposed to be in this world, and the success you achieve every day in facing and defeating your saboteurs.

That's the whole reason for being here in this world. YOU are here to bring forth your unique vision that NO ONE else has inside of them.

The Vision Scope

The Vision Scope shows you a world without fear in it's Tell-A-Vision.
How does it work? By earning all 8 clueberries by defeating saboteurs, using tools and building your character.
Check out The Clueberry Social Emotional Learning Game to learn more.

What is a Saboteur?

In Clueberry World, a saboteur is a made up creature of the mind that represents a negative thought or mindset in ourselves and others.

The core principles in Clueberry World empower you to understand fourteen different kinds of saboteurs, the emotional baggage they present to you and how to respond to overcome these saboteurs.

It's important to understand how saboteurs work because negative thoughts create negative emotions which often lead to negative behavior. By being aware of your thoughts and emotions, you then have the power to create a positive, healthy mindset, regardless of what's unfolding in your life.

Sabotaging thoughts come from inner confusion or fear within ourselves or in others. In Clueberry World, you will learn to see that these fear-based thoughts all take on a unique form, have a unique voice and use a unique method for their sabotage. This process of acquainting yourself with forms of self-sabotage will enable you to become emotionally strong because you will begin to build your own personal tool box to handle these saboteurs when they show up. Clueberry World is the training ground for you to develop a language to respond to situations in your real life.

Clueberry World empowers you to understand inner and outer saboteurs, because everything goes awry when you let them get the best of you and affect your self-esteem and self-image, which then affects your self statements, decisions and choices. Think about it. How will self-doubt or self-criticism keep you from raising your hand in class, asking for help, or being comfortable trying new things?

The ultimate goal of Clueberry World is to explore the relationship between thoughts, feelings, beliefs, behavior and choices, in order to empower you to see you are capable of more than you ever thought possible.

Meet the
DOUBT DRAGON

The Doubt Dragon lives in a Series of Staircases to Nowhere. He stands over your shoulder and whispers, "Be unsure of yourself" over and over. This is dangerous because he will keep saying it until you believe him!

The Doubt Dragon intends to start a fire of disbelief in you. If you don't believe in yourself with great strength, he knows that one spark of doubt can cause you to totally crumble. He tries to cause one spark of doubt inside you because that's all he needs. Be careful with the Doubt Dragon. He's subtle in his ways...often simply making a face that shows you he's doubtful or he may say: "I don't know about that...." or "Well, I am not sure you can do that...."

Then he'll stand back and watch as you blow on the doubtful thought, transforming it into a large flame. He will laugh, because in trying to put out the spark you begin to fan the flames, causing the fire to spread. The expression "fight fire with fire", doesn't apply in this case! Don't fight doubt because it only causes even more doubt.

You'll fill your whole self up with thick dark smoky question marks. Then what? Then you can be trapped off track, barely able to put one foot in front of other. That's how he derails you, paralyzes you and keeps you going up and down the Staircases to Nowhere.

You know the Doubt Dragon's derailed you if you are unsure, uncertain or questioning yourself in a way that's causing you to be paralyzed. He's trying to keep you from making a decision, taking any action or taking a step forward. However, sometimes doubt is good. Call to your mind different times you paused to doubt yourself and it helped you make a better decision going forward.

QUALM

Qualms are coins given out by The Doubt Dragon as emotional baggage. It says "In Doubt We Trust" because being doubtful of yourself means you are not trusting yourself!

So what is its power? You find yourself suddenly surrounded in a fog of uncertainty filled with question marks as this powerful coin radiates confusion and uncertainty all around you.

Like all Saboteurs, sometimes The Doubt Dragon stuffs his baggage in your backpack without you even knowing. It happens like this: you are on the Train of Thought, happily propelling forward and suddenly you are derailed by self doubt. This is when you know you are going to find a Qualm...or 2 or 3 inside your backpack! Don't forget that taking baggage from a Saboteur means you have been derailed by a negative encounter. So how do you know you are being weighed down and thrown off track by having too many Qualms in your backpack?

Okay, here's how you get Qualms. It is tricky, so listen up. First, doubt showed up in some form. Remember, you have a Doubt Dragon inside you, but when someone else doubts you, that's their inner Doubt Dragon showing up in them. Second, you didn't recognize this experience as doubt. This one's important. The whole purpose of Clueberry World is to CLUE YOU IN to thoughts and emotions. Why? Just knowing what you're dealing with makes you aware, which weakens it's power over you. Learn to say: "Oh that's just my inner Doubt Dragon!" This leads to the third thing. If you don't have a CLUE what's going on in you, you end up carrying that feeling with you after the moment is over. You carry that moment into your next encounter with a friend or teacher, into your next day, even into the next week, month or year. This is the experience of walking around with Qualms in life.

Now you are clued in to the Qualm baggage, so you can drop it! To start, begin to recall moments when doubt thoughts rose up in your mind.

How to Respond

What's the opposite of being doubtful of yourself? Being certain.

So, when you've been dragged into derailing doubt by the Doubt Dragon, here's how you realign with the Train of Thought: respond with CERTAINTY.

See, the curious thing about a Doubt Dragon is that they shrink when unabashed certainty is directed back their way. Certainty is like a fire hose hose that cools down doubt. When the Doubt Dragon overwhelms your mind with his fire breathing fog of question marks, watch as your certainty statement acts like a powerful stream of cool water that clears the air and helps you see the way back on track.

Here's the thing: at first, your certainty feels made up and false. You may repeat over and over again, "I do not doubt myself," for instance which is a certainty statement in the negative. In the beginning when you are just learning about the power of certainty statements, be sure they are in the affirmative. Here are some certainty statements in the affirmative that are even more powerful:

"I trust myself."
"I am certain."
"I know I can do it."
"I believe this is all for the best."
 "I believe in me."

The Doubt Dragon responds to certainty like a cockroach in daylight. He will run and hide into the darkness.

Your response to the Doubt Dragon will eventually become automatic and easy. Being certain of yourself and knowing when to listen to good doubt (a thoughtful pause) takes practice.

Meet the
CRITICAL WARTMONGER

The Critical Wartmonger, feeling deeply as if there is something wrong with herself, seeks to draw your attention from being your best self or following your dream by implanting the false idea that there is something wrong with you as well. This makes her feel better.

She sabotages by picking and picking at you with cruel, biting comments. On the outside she may appear large, but she behaves like a relentless mosquito trying to nip away at your confidence. She relates well with the Bullies in this way. However, when they get together, the conversation is a tennis match of fault finding with each other because both are interested in the same thing: shaking your confidence.

The Critical Wartmonger knows that you may confuse "being confident" with "being arrogant." She knows people are always afraid of sounding conceited or stuck up to their friends. Her greatest trick is preying on your own fear that being confident is egotistical. She often convinces you that if you don't believe her, then you'll be too confident which will lead to people being intimidated by you or you appearing too stuck up.

The Critical Wartmonger is trying to challenge your confidence by throwing you daily challenges in the form of your own inner critic or in the form of someone else's criticism. Confidence is not arrogance. It's the courage to overlook all the "why not's" in order to say, "I am willing to try," or "I may not be 100% sure about myself, but I believe I'll figure it out as things come." Building confidence is the daily practice of being aware of your faults but instead of letting them determine the outcome, choosing to trust in yourself anyway.

Forgive her. She's got a hard job of trying to make you feel you have no confidence! She is obviously destined for arthritis, pointing her finger at people all day long, never mind all the wrinkles she'll have from furrowing her brows in disapproval...

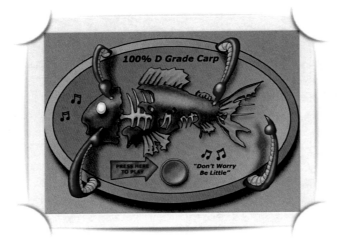

D GRADE CARP

Would you want to carry around a rotten fish with scorpion stingers that plays "Don't Worry Be Little" all day long? Well, if you allow the Critical Wartmonger to get to you, distract you and derail you, you've chosen to take her baggage: a D Grade Carp...ewwww.

Carp is another word for faultfinding and nitpicking. Think about what "fault finding" means. It means you are actively engaged in looking for faults. Think about what "nitpicking" means. It literally means to find something small and pick at it. Neither of these are worthwhile mental activities!

This train of thought leaves a bad feeling because it reduces a person, an idea or an experience to a small fault and discounts the whole picture. No one wants to feel cheated out of the whole picture or be defined by one small fault. It causes an emotional experience of being degraded, small, or stung.

Think of this smelly, rotten, stinging, annoyingly repetitive singing fish as a reminder! D Grade Carp reminds you what it feels like to engage in negative criticism is to look for faults, find them and then start picking at them. It also reminds you that when you criticize someone else, you have turned into a green wartmonger who gives out rotten fish with stingers to people! Is that who you want to be?

Didn't think so....

How to Respond

The thing to remember is this: even if you were 100% perfect, which nobody is, the Critical Wartmonger will invent something to criticize. Even if what she says seems true, which it often will, focus on making light of it. Show as much CONFIDENCE as you can.

First ask yourself, "Is this criticism helpful or hurtful?" We all have an inner critic and other people have an inner critic. When you start to recognize the voice of your inner critic or someone else's inner critic, it's important to discern where that voice is coming from. To figure it out, simply consider "Do I feel good or bad? Is this experience a Critical Wartmonger trying to derail me?" You will know you've encountered a Critical Wartmonger in yourself or from another person if you feel degraded, rotten or stung, whereas helpful criticism brings on a feeling of reflection and pause. Helpful criticism helps you grow.

If the criticism is hurtful, point out your perfections, because The Critical Wartmonger attempts to loudly point out your imperfections. How? Simply begin listing all the perfectly perfect good things about yourself from your perfect smile to all the great things you're good at. This energy will cause her to go pale. (Pale kale green is not a good look on an ogre! Promise, she'll shrink away.)

Joke with The Critical Wartmonger by making light of her biting comments. Making light of a painful comment is NOT easy, but this can reduce the sting of her words and soothe the bite for you. The purpose is for YOU to use these experiences as an opportunity to respond from your best self. If you don't, then you have allowed the Critical Wartmonger to give you her baggage! Consider when someone criticizes your appearance, your idea or a mistake you made. How can you respond so that the thoughts coming from someone else's Critical Wartmonger don't become the thoughts of your inner critic?

Meet the
UGLY WARTMONGER

Simply put, The Ugly Wartmonger is ignorant.

Every encounter with the Ugly Wartmonger is a nasty encounter because he lacks insight and perspective. As a result, most of what he says is devoid of compassion and a sweeping, and usually a bias unfair judgement.

None of us know EVERYTHING but what makes this guy different is he doesn't even know that he doesn't know what he doesn't know. Did you get that?

The Ugly Wartmonger looks kind of scary and big but really he is weak. You will never ever catch him admitting he's wrong because he sees it as a sign of weakness. Because of this, he goes to great lengths to defend his opinions. This is another thing he doesn't know: that it's actually a sign of strength, not weakness to admit you don't know all the answers, and that's something he's not capable of. He causes a lot of pain because he will grab onto a couple tidbits of information and spew out hateful words and comments to compensate for his lack of insight and perspective.

He is so highly negative. He's full of "can'ts" and "why not's". He will huff and puff and well, in short, he's all around got a really closed up mind. Because he is so limited in his knowledge, he tends to identify with an outdated set of principles. He is very rigid and cannot think outside of the structure he subscribes to, so he is always talking about right or wrong in relation to this one structure.

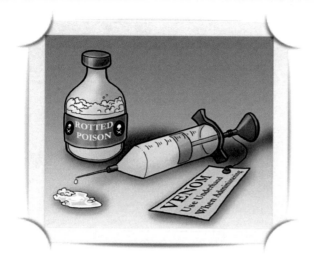

VENOM

noun.//toxin

Have you ever felt poisoned by a person, idea or experience? If so, then you had an encounter with an Ugly Wartmonger! The Ugly Wartmonger is full of causes toxicity. You will feel contaminated by the experience.

What does it feel like to get shot with 100% pure toxins straight into your blood stream? You became infected. The Ugly Wartmonger doesn't share or exchange thoughts and ideas. He transmits his memes through injection, and that's why you are left to feel like you just contracted a diseased meme. Memes are ideas or principles that are passed throughout a culture. They can be good or bad. However, the Ugly Wartmonger intends to spread memes that are hateful, polarizing and greatly judgmental.

We have all been infected by a toxic idea or meme from the Ugly Wartmonger. Many problems in society are caused by toxic memes passed on by the Ugly Wartmonger. The easiest way to recognize you are encountering ignorance is to check in with how you feel in the encounter or experience. If you feel injected with toxicity, then you know you are dealing with ignorance.

Ignorance causes all kinds of problems, sometimes unintentionally. The Ugly Wartmonger could even cause damage unintentionally. Examples of this are when you make a mistake or misjudge a situation because you had limited knowledge of the facts.

HOW TO RESPOND

The opposite of ignorance is knowledge. The #1 thing to remember is that all ignorance comes from a lack of knowledge, so that means the Ugly Wartmonger will always lack insight and perspective. The Ugly Wartmonger thinks in limited terms: right and wrong, us and them, and feel threatened by anything or anyone that challenges his limited understanding of the world.

Show don't tell. You may try to respond by telling The Ugly Wartmonger your insights and perspectives but you can bet he will resist being told how to think and what to think. Remember his whole reality is based on a rigid set of really outdated principles. So, instead of telling the Ugly Wartmonger your perspective, show him. One way to show him is to note commonalities between your ideas and his ideas, in other words how people are more the same than different. In this way, you are subtly guiding him to a broader, more unifying understanding of the world.

The Ugly Wartmonger can be extremely dangerous if pushed too hard. They are highly defensive and see opportunities to defend their principles as a way they can reinforce their loyalty to what they represent. Never try to pry open an already closed mind. Opened minded people are always open to closed minded people but close minded people never return the favor. The Ugly Wartmonger's entire identity or sense of self is based on a closed set of principles as: it makes him feel safe. When you challenge his principles, you are literally challenging how he makes sense of the world.

Instead of reflecting or considering how he can think in a new way, he will see YOU as the cause of his discomfort. This means he's not ready and you need to move on or stay away. It's not your job to open his mind. Remember, you are only responsible for being aware of what you are encountering.

Meet the
WORRY WARTMONGER

The Worry Wartmonger is positively terrified of the unknown and the unforeseen.

She spends her days yapping about what might be, when it might be, and whose fault it would be might it be or could be. Her voice scrapes across every situation with the same irritating pitch. She will not let you get a word in edgewise. She is distantly related to the Doubt Dragon since her aim is to paralyze you with the infinite possibilities of what if's.

Oddly, her trick is that she almost always makes sense. Sometimes it may seem she has a good point here and there. This may encourage you to entertain her ideas for a little while. Only in hindsight do you recognize that time spent with her was truly a complete waste of time.

She feels her job is to tell you all the things that could go wrong so you can start your worrying in advance. She will convince you that it's irresponsible NOT to worry, and that worrying is a way to show yourself or other people how much you care are about someone or something. Of course this is just a trick! It's a way she tries to pull you into her low level mindset and keep you distracted from being on track. Her whole motivation is to concern and alarm you through distraction. Think about how easy you've made it for her in the past by considering how many times you've worried about something that turned out to be no big deal.

VEX

noun.//angst

Vex is another word for worry which causes angst and will often cause an upset stomach! The baggage for the Worry Wartmonger is a fizzy drink made with fresh brouhaha, artificial hubbub syrup and partially hydrogenated fingernails floating on top. It's called Vex. Yuck!

When you spend too much time listening to and identifying with the Worry Wartmonger, and allowing her thoughts to become yours, you will end up drinking Vex. Worry is filled with artificial ingredients.

Artificial means fake or not real and soda is filled with synthetic, manmade ingredients that are derived from unnatural sources. This means that you are literally processing her manufactured ideas. You are ingesting and digesting worries based in something artificial: fear.

HOW TO RESPOND

It's helpful to ask "Is it true right now?" This simple question disarms the power of The Worry Wartmonger because she know's the answer is NO! She wants to see you frowning, furrowing your eyebrows in concern, and biting your fingernails so treat her lightly: give a smile, or a lighthearted wave.

Imagine the best. Worrying is imagining the worst and engages your imagination in a negative way by painting a picture of what could go wrong. Instead of imagining the worst, use your imagination to picture the best! The Worry Wartmonger causes worries because she thinks worrying will prevent bad things from happening if there is enough. Comical, isn't it? This is so far from the true. Often, worrying is the actual cause of a bad outcome. Worriers also think that worrying will show others how much they care about a situation. Caring about a situation through worry is misguided. Worrying does not help or advance any situation in any way possible. True caring for a situation is supporting it with a positive, trusting and faith filled attitude.

Worry can be helpful. The Worry Wartmonger's job is to derail you from feeling good about yourself, your abilities, your dreams, your accomplishments, your future, your past and your present. Worry is helpful when it keeps us from making a bad decision or from hurting ourselves or others. Call to mind instances when worry can be helpful if it results in protecting you or keeping you safe.

Meet the
DRONE GIANT

Dodger, avoider, quitter, bum, slouch, loafer, shirker, maligerer...all these words describe this big oaf who sits on a stool all day at Coffee and Dronuts.

He rambles, he rants, he starts every sentence with "if I was in charge" and "how'd I do things" but never suggests an idea rooted in his own experience. He feels constantly wronged and is forever insisting he is being taken advantage of...the Drone Giant has major trust issues!

The Drone Giant makes some convincing arguments and loops and is forever trying to stall your in pursuit of action. He has, as the saying goes, a lot of bark and no bite. He doesn't have any intention of taking action while he feeds off his audience who all sit around him and validate how unfair life is, how wrong things are, how crooked everyone is, complaint after complaint after complaint.

The predominant mindset of the Drone Giant is to perseverate on outdated ideas because he is out of touch with the current times. Instead of accepting times have changed and innovative solutions are required to create solutions, he will drone on about how things used to be and whose fault things are the way they are now.

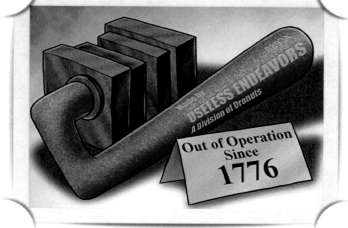

IDLER

This rusty old piece of an engine is the baggage of the Drone Giant because it serves no purpose, it's use is outdated, and it does nothing to add to your current circumstances. The effect of the Drone Giant is to weigh you down with all his useless endeavors and outdated ideas. He will trap you into focusing on a problem and who caused the problem instead of accepting old systems need updating and new solutions are required to serve the ever evolving needs of people and society.

Sometimes, when the Drone Giant shows up in others, he will resort into a victim mentality because he sees himself as the victim of the times or a victim of younger generations who don't understand what "it was like when he was younger." When he shows up in you, it's because you are set on telling an old story about your past, going over facts and story lines about old victim stories that you want to validate having caused your current circumstances. When you engage with a Drone Giant in yourself or in another, and end up feeling weighed down, hopeless about the state of things, and overwhelmed with the enormity of society's problems, he has succeeded in giving you a giant, heavy Idler to carry around...and that's no fun!

HOW TO RESPOND

Drone Giants are a unique kind of saboteur. If you encounter one in someone else, it is often best to simply focus on the awareness you have identified which saboteur you are dealing with. Staying present to your own awareness is a powerful tool for remaining in your own power and not at the affect of his negativity as he drones on and on. What you are accomplishing seems like almost nothing because in a sense you are not responding at all but no response to a Drone Giant is a response because his goal is to hook you into agreeing with him. Any nod of your head, or joining in on the conversation fuels him and causes you to be further invested, and further sucked into his emphasis on problems, of victimhood, along with distorted perception of the facts, or stories from the past.

If you encounter a Drone Giant in yourself, you are choosing to engage in old facts and stories from the past that are no longer serving you. If something is no longer functioning to serve you, whether it's a story, mistake, time period in your life you regret or miss, or a mindset, you are encountering a Drone Giant. The Drone Giant is all about bringing up what no longer serves you and always, always, always that's something he is bringing up from the past.

This inner saboteur has a trick up his sleeve: he not only focuses on negative or old ways of the past, but he also creates nostalgia and longing for a time that is long over. Reminiscing on the past is a healthy an beautiful practice when it's honoring good memories and celebrating personal progress. Longing for the past when it's inhibiting growth in the present, causing close-mindedness to change or resistance to seeing yourself or the world in a new way is the Drone Giant trying to derail you.

THE APATHETIC CATS

The Apathetic Alley Cats express their ambivalence by being lazy. Plain and simple.

They are chronically bored because they have not found anything to be inspired, passion or enthused about. They are simply indifferent.

They may see both sides, but don't feel strongly about anything in particular. Occasionally, they venture off the Progress Plateau towards the Lazy Maze where they spend most of their time.

They try to entice you by making their lives out to be comfortable and easy. It may appear completely harmless to hang out with them. Apathetic Alley Cats are extremely difficult to resist! Their apparent harmlessness is how they fool you into becoming apathetic. They always appear exhausted, or worn out but have exerted no real work. Everything is too much for them. They are masters of avoidance by filling up their day with whatever they can to appear busy. They don't strain themselves ever and are big into passive activities that give them a sense of accomplishment such as appointments for grooming, or creating a schedule for napping or cleaning something that's already clean.

Apathy is contagious! They are the perfect example of "You are the company you keep." Hang around apathy, you become apathetic. Apathy is a powerless fuel. You will not make it to the Vision Machine running on apathy.

TICKETS

When you start to feel wishy washy and experience a loss of interest in things that used to inspire you or get you amped up, consider yourself stuck with the Apathetic Alley Cat's baggage: bad seats.

You are in full blown motivation meltdown, and you've reached the point where nothing can rev your inspiration engines to catapult you to engaging in previously enjoyed activities. Where you used to care, used to be willing to activate your inner yeehaw for an interesting new adventure, your inner woohoo when you engage in some healthy competition, or enjoy taking a stand with an impassioned argument around one of your favorite topics of injustice...now, nothing can get your heart racing and your adrenaline flowing.

Apathy is an experience of being on the fence, unable to make a decision and stuck in a state of not even caring that you don't care. That's the uncomfortable part: not the bad seats...but the fact that you don't even care to try for a better view of life.

Ambivalence and apathy are caused by an internal disconnect between your heart and mind, and can cause all sorts of problems such as procrastination, allowing things to go wrong and watching without taking action or intervening, a lack of compassion or an indifferent attitude.

APATHETIC
ALLEY CATS

HOW TO RESPOND

If you encounter an Alley Cat in the middle of your inspiring speech about your vision or idea, don't keep trying to inspire the Alley Cat and whatever you do, don't take their blank stare and disinterest personally. Alley Cats are asleep on the inside even if their eyes are open. Apathetic Alley Cats also appear disinterested when they don't understand something - they will have a blank stare. It's easy to take it personally and get your feelings hurt around an Alley Cat because their sheer indifference is quite insulting. It's a trick of the Alley Cats to try and cause you to be wish washy with yourself. They act so disinterested in you that you begin to become dismissive about what you're passionate about. Apathetic Alley Cats are always trying to make laziness look cool, to cover up the fact that they are in fact afraid to stand behind anything in life. While it's always painful and insulting to be rejected, remain in your inspiration and committed to your endeavor because the Alley Cats would love to see you abandon your goals and sense of purpose. Don't judge the quality and merit of your endeavors, ideas and goals based on the reaction (or lack of a reaction) from an Alley Cat! Being enthusiastic and excited about life is something the cats will try and suck out of you thus causing you to lose your motivation. Their ultimate goal is to make you want to give up and join them in a life of not caring.

Realign with your passion. When you are around Apathetic Alley Cats, they tend to drain you. You are left feeling you need to be uplifted or that your inner spark needs to be re-ignited. Realigning with your sense of "why" is how to move from apathy to passion. Your why is your sense of purpose, what you stand for, what you believe in, what you envision yourself achieving or the goal you have set for yourself. Focus on the qualities you need to cultivate in yourself in order to achieve your goals and become the person you envision. This practice activates an inner power that brings about the feeling of clarity, the energy of inspiration and the enthusiasm to proceed with the next steps towards achieving your desired outcomes. The Apathetic Alley Cats are by nature great at pretending to allow you into their cool little club, but in truth under the surface don't have your best interest at heart and are only trying to use you to validate their own lazy existence.

THE BULLIES

You can encounter a bully in someone else or in yourself. Encountering a bully in someone else is usually a harsh, brutal and cruel experience. It's a total takedown of your self esteem because you are left feeling attacked just for being YOU.

Bullies often seek out unique people who have some special quality that intimidates them. For instance, someone who is especially talented at something activates the bully in another person because bullies want power. If you have power, then their aim becomes to diminish you. Sometimes, you can be targeted for no apparent reason by a bully and suddenly you feel thrown on a stage with an unwanted spotlight blinding you in front of a jeering snickering audience. Encountering a bully is an experience that causes you to want to shrink in size, hide behind the curtain of life and just disappear. It leaves you feeling your very existence is being rejected, that you are somehow abnormal and that there is something wrong with you to be targeted.

The effect of encountering a bully can be you are left feeling very sad, very low, and even feeling some self hatred. It's a bad track to be on leading to feelings of isolation, that you are misunderstood, and distancing yourself from friends and family. Bully encounters are very painful because it's rejection from your peers in a public setting. Fear of this kind of humiliation is the #1 fear of so many bullies themselves, which is why they project and play out their exact fear onto you.

CANON
BALL

The baggage of the Bullies is an explosive device because when you feel bullied, pressure begins to build up inside of you. Every encounter with a bully adds more and more pressure inside. What eventually happens is that something unrelated will often cause you to explode.

You find yourself blowing up at everyone around you (or the people who you care about and who care about you). It's usually something small that causes you the final explosion. You blow up over a little spat with a sibling, a bad grade on a test, not making a team, someone bumps into you in the hallway, or your best friend doesn't want to sit with you on the bus. Bully encounters basically cause you to become a mine field and everyone around you is in danger of detonating you..

Like all saboteurs, you can encounter a bully in someone else or in yourself. A Bully encounter is like a chain reaction of events. Someone is bullied, they become emotionally weighed down causing them to become explosive, a human mine field of sorts, so they relieve this pressure by giving it to someone else in the only way that seems rational to them: by bullying someone else. In that sense, it's a very vicious circle.

MR. & MRS BULLY

HOW TO RESPOND

Bullies have some basic tactics they all use and understanding them will help guide you in how to respond. The purpose of Clueberry World is to empower you to understand how YOU will respond. This doesn't mean you actually are face to face with a saboteur. It's the process of responding to yourself, sometimes. You know a bully is bullying you so they can manage their own inner explosives. That said, you can't change anyone but yourself. Bullies, like the Angry Android, can be very dangerous. Your goal is to protect yourself, to be safe, and to minimize the damage to yourself.

A Bully encounter is like a chain reaction of events. Someone is bullied, they become emotionally weighed down causing them to become explosive, a human mine field of sorts, so they relieve this pressure by giving it to someone else in the only way that seems rational to them: by bullying someone else. Tormenting to teasing, intimidating to oppressing, annoying pest to rowdy and rough...bullying takes many forms. You cannot change a bully, only keep the bully's tactics from giving you emotional baggage. That's your ultimate goal.

First of all, let's face it. In life, the experiences that carry the greatest stakes for our social life have the potential to cause the greatest degree of emotional damage to self esteem and self worth. Bullying tops the cake in the area of potentially causing full scale self destruction because it causes humiliation in public at a time when messages are coming from all directions that you should base your self worth on your popularity, the number of friends you have, and how well you fit in. Bullying causes you to feel like an outcast, the exact opposite of all these messages. So how do you survive this experience? It has to STOP. That's first.

You will learn that a long lasting sense of self worth is based on YOUR own definition of cool. You may not be ready to accept it wasn't your fault. Self acceptance is a gift you have to give yourself.

THE EXAGGERATION OX

The Exaggeration Ox has a very important job of delivering news to the world. He has a HUGE influence on how people receive information and he shapes how they perceive facts. How does he do this? When an event or news worthy story is written, he will choose very carefully how he presents the story and what order the information is delivered in. He also looks at what stories he wants people to pay the most attention to, and then places them accordingly in the newspaper. The front page is for stories or events that he is asking the public to pay the most attention to. This would be a perfectly fine system if the Exaggeration Ox didn't have to make money for his newspaper! Why? He makes an association between how much MORE money he will make if the story is placed in such a way that the public reacts in order to bring in more revenue. For example, a story about the weather can cause the public to race out and stock up on water and canned food goods. Companies know this and advertise accordingly. The news has to the power to ultimately drive the behavior of the public, which then creates patterns in society.

What does this mean for you and the Exaggeration Ox? In order for the newspaper to be of any value, he must capture and retain the attention of the public. In order to do that, The Ox reduces himself to all sorts of tacts. For example, he often puts hogwash in the news, simply to embellish the details of news to make events more interesting and captivating to an audience. He glorifies negative, sad or tragic events to hook your attention. He knows people are attracted to the heightened feeling of dramatic events and even will create a controversy where none previously existed simply to reel in an audience. Also he glamorizes unhealthy images to sell products. Being aware of this empowers you.

HOGWASH

Hogwash is the baggage of the Exaggeration Ox. You know you've been fed hogwash if have bought into something that changed your priorities in an unhealthy way or make an unhealthy decision based on something you read in the newspaper.

The Ox is motivated to help you form an opinion, and he will create hype or inflate a sense of urgency in order to activate your reaction. The hogwash he adds to news stories is often for the purpose of creating fear in the public.

The effect is usually a state of powerlessness because the Ox knows people who feel powerless are weakened in their ability to think for themselves. If you feel alarmed, attracted to the hype, overwhelmed with powerlessness, you have been fed the Ox's hogwash.

Examples of being fed hogwash are watching advertisements that make you feel incomplete if you don't have the product advertised. Causing you to feel incomplete is a tactic of the Ox. He knows that if he can make you feel like you can't live without something, or that some product or service will be the answer to your happiness, you will go buy it. Similarly, if the Ox reports news or events in a way that incites fear or causes you to feel certain emotions, you will be driven to behave according to his agenda.

HOW TO RESPOND

The Ox has certain ways of crafting the news, such as ordering facts in a certain way. Why does he do this? The order in which information is presented is the order that you will then process the information. What he wants you to pay the most attention to will appear in the headline. The headline also will clue you into how he wants you THINK about the story he is about to tell you. For example, once a study was done by Clueberry World that gave 3 different people the same exact story written by the Ox. The story was about a boy who climbed a tree trying to save his cat. The only difference was each story had a different headline. One headline read Courageous Boy Climbs Tree to Save Cat, another read, Boy Found in Tree Mother Nowhere to be Found, and the third headline said, Tree Climbing Cat Raises New Questions Over Fence Debate.

The reason the Ox is called the Exaggeration Ox is because he will literally exaggerate one detail of a story and create a headline that aims to grab your attention and shape how you think. How you think about a certain news story then heavily influences 3 key factors in your ability to maintain a positive sense of personal empowerment. One, news stories have the power to shape the attitudes you create about yourself, people, places and things. Two, news stories have the power to shape the conclusions you make. Three, news stories have the power to effect the connections you make. In a sense, the news media has the power to influence your overall understanding and perception of your place in the world!

Remember, the source of all self esteem stems from your ability to have power over your thoughts and emotions at any given moment. Notice how a news story can instantly cause emotions in you. Be aware and informed. Question the motive or intention behind the information you are receiving. Note whether you feel powerless or empowered, desperation or inspiration. Noticing how you feel gives you the ability to decide what you want to buy into.

THE INSINCERITY OGRE

The Insincerity Ogre gives you the brush off. Often when you are excited about something new, or inspired with a new idea, you want to share it with everyone. Why? Because you want people to say, "wow that's a great idea!" or "I believe in you!" or "Let me know whatever I can do to help you with that!"

We all want acceptance for our ideas and beliefs. When you are uncertain of where you stand or you feel insecure in your beliefs, you look for someone to provide that stamp of approval. Because you are not feeling strong and need someone to give you that stamp of approval, you are disempowering yourself. The Insincerity Ogre squashes you with his lack of authenticity. You can sense when someone truly believes in you and the moment you open yourself up to someone who is giving you the brush off, notice how you feel. You will probably feel deflated, vulnerable, scared, worried, nervous, regretful, embarrassed and shut down. That's because you are literally giving your power away to someone else to determine what YOU are capable of. No one can define what you are capable of...except YOU.

The Insincerity Ogre is very damaging to your self esteem because he carries on as if he will follow through his statement of support in the way of resources, or becoming part of helping you in some way or provide you some level of support. When he doesn't follow through, you crumble, because you have allowed someone else to determine the value of your idea or endeavor. He doesn't care he hurt you. He's too busy inflating someone else with a false sense of support.

SPAM

The baggage of the Insincerity Ogre is a fake version of ham because he leaves you feeling the same way that processed foods with artificial ingredients make you feel. While they tend to promise they will deliver something comparable to the real thing, they never do. Actually, they never taste as good as the real thing and never provide the nourishment that only something that is authentic can provide.

Spam pretends to be ham, just like the Insincerity Ogre pretends to be authentic. If you are tricked into being inflated with empty promises, you will ended up weighed down by the baggage of the Insincerity Ogre on Progress Plateau.

HOW TO RESPOND

See The Insincerity Ogre as a teacher. He is there to remind you over and over, as many times as it takes, about the experience of disappointment that you will feel when you allow someone else's reaction to define how YOU feel about yourself. Without fail, the experience of consuming something artificial will bring about major disappointment and truthfully, disappointment can be a very painful emotional experience.

Choose who you share your intimate desires, dreams and visions. Choose people who you can trust not to judge you. However if they DO judge you, remember your goal is to not let the opinions of others, the insincere comments or the brush off by someone who you look up to, determine how you proceed in your life.

Just like the Exaggeration Ox has the power to influence how you think about the news IF YOU ALLOW him to, the Insincerity Ogre has the power to influence how you think about your ideas and endeavors...but only if you ALLOW him to.

You may encounter many Insincerity Ogres in your life, and they will consistently trap you into appearing as though they care about your passions, only to later disappoint you in some way. Sometimes Insincerity Ogres don't reveal themselves right away. You find out they laughed at you behind your back, or gossiped about you, or simply never cared and you become deflated and disappointed. Always empower yourself by viewing this experience as a reinforcement that it's up to YOU to believe you can do it.

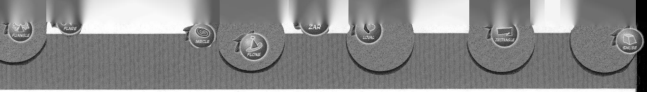

THE ANXIETY ANDROID

Encountering the Anxiety Android feels like something has swooped down and rested heavily on your shoulders. If you wait too long to respond or react to him, he will attempt to fill you with more and more anxiety. His pressure gets worse with every second that passes.

He wants to make you feel so heavy that you fall to your knees and have trouble breathing.

The Anxiety Android works in 3 phases (if you let him go on too long). **First**, he says whatever he can to present the absolute worst possible scenario or outcome. **Second,** he will paint the picture of the worst possible scenario or outcome in a very convincing vivid illustration. **Finally,** comes the big performance. He begins huffing and puffing, heaving and hoeing. Sweating and wringing his hands, he scratches his scalp. Pointing out his hives, pulling out his hair, twisting his lips, and pointing to his dried out tongue all in response to his now believing the absolute truth of his vivid illustration of the worst possible outcome.

Basically, the Anxiety Android **disarms you by alarming you**. It can be so severe, you actually have a physical reaction. He rattles your nervous system causing physical symptoms that escalate in your body until you feel paralyzed and unable to function.

BASKET CASE

The baggage of the Anxiety Android is a basket case because this is what you become when he has taken you over.

The experience of being a basket case is that you have lost all composure. Composure is being grounded, emotional stable and in total self control. Becoming a basket case means you are now a human container for nervous energy, causing you to be closed up and closed off from using your mind to gain clarity and your body to take action.

A basket case is the experience of tightly winding yourself up with the unknowns, what if's and worst possible scenarios. This is when a single thought based in fear of the future or a scenario that is unlikely, becomes a full blown, full scale reality in the mind and elicits an emotional response of flight or fight in the primal part of the brain. When this happens, the cognitive and logical functions of the brain that de-escalate fear are overridden and become paralyzed. Any tactics, such as strategies to calm yourself, become difficult to access because a physical response has taken over for self preservation.

When the Anxiety Android turns us into a basket case, you are in danger of now being closed off and become unavailable to hearing, listening, and seeking resources or help.

HOW TO

RESPOND

Once you turn into a basket case, activate all the power you have inside your mind and body. Anxiety tends to "close in," and in doing so, closes you off from using your mind to talk yourself into clarity and gain perspective. Your body freezes up. Emotion is often called energy in motion. That's because strong emotions such as anxiety have the ability to affect every part of your being, from thoughts to behavior to actions. The entry and exit point for your emotional energy can be controlled by simply beware aware of your own breathing.

Whether you are facing your own inner Anxiety Android or an Anxiety Android in someone else, the response is to breathe. Breathing is automatic, so you tend to forget it contains an enormous power to control your emotional state. Slow, deep breathing can calm your anxious feelings allowing them to flow right out of you. This also happens with exercise causing fast breathing. You will completely flush out heavy, sticky emotions. Take several quick breaths using your core stomach muscles, then take several deep breaths, the several long slow breaths and repeat. Because anxiety often paralyzes you to take the actions you know you could take such as exercise, or tackling a chore to break up the rotten energy. Be careful because sometimes more anxiety is piled on if you beat yourself up for not doing what you "should" or "could" be doing to make yourself feel better.

That's why it's best to use a controlled breathing exercise as a method to control anxiety because it requires the least amount of effort to move out of the state of anxiety. Also, by controlling your breathing, you are guiding yourself to remember you are empowered to be in control of everything in your life, including your strong emotions like anxiety.

THE ANGRY ANDROID

As with all the saboteurs, you can encounter The Angry Android in yourself or in the presence of another person. His anger starts out as frustration and escalates and escalates, strengthening its hold over you.

The most extreme degree of anger can be dangerous because it has a blinding effect. You literally lose your vision because you lose sight of what's important. Vision is the anchor to inner self control because you lose sight of consequences to your words and actions. This means you can potentially inflict emotional or physical damage to yourself or others. This is how the Angry Android causes you to lose control of yourself.

The Angry Android can appear only mildly angry one moment, but within seconds, his temper has shot through the roof. In a rage, he cannot see where his hands are flailing or who they are flailing at. He cannot stand up straight or even breath evenly. He is simply trying to relieve himself of tension, which you can literally see blowing out of every orifice of his body. When the tension is all blown out he comes to and is usually quite surprised by the damage he has caused around him.

With great zest and gusto, he stands over a boiling pot, stewing all day. Often he lets a soup stew too long. He is known for a dish everybody can smell a mile away: Bitter Beets. With all the energy he outputs, sometimes it's even possible you can get addicted to being around the drama of an Angry Android.

BITTER BEETS

Bitter Beets are literally bottled up anger. The Angry Android leaves you with a bitter taste in your mouth. When you hang out too long with the Angry Android, you will end up getting an acidic, sharp, flavor filling up your senses and leaving you with a not so lovely look on your face.

Bitter Beets will weigh you down and keep you stuck in an angry state of mind. Carrying the Bitter Beets makes you crabby, testy, and cranky. You become short tempered easily. Bitter Beets let off the stench of something aged for too long and sometimes this causes you to appear like you are constantly smelling something unpleasant! Your overall appearance and attitude deteriorate when you are carrying Bitter Beets. You will find yourself will repel positive people and circumstances.

HOW TO RESPOND

There is a difference between passion and anger. Anger channeled properly can transform into positive energy and become the fuel for passionate action. Anger is a powerful emotion that moves through your body. If it's strong enough, it can stunt your ability to process logically. This is why the #1 response to anger is to lose control or lose your temper. Anger is paralyzing.

Your #1 priority when encountering your inner Angry Android or someone else's Angry Android is to focus on ONE thought: "An Angry Android is trying to control me and I will not allow him to." Repeating this keeps you separate from IDENTIFYING with and therefore, resonating with the Angry Android. You hold him at a distance with this statement. It's a highly effective way to allow the emotion of anger to move through you without bottling it up and expressing it through negative words, actions and behaviors. It takes practice. Every time you repeat this sentence and successfully calm yourself degree by degree, lowering the temperature of anger within yourself, you are learning the art of mastering one of the most powerful saboteurs in Clueberry World.

Control is the key. He tries to cause you to LOSE control, and the truth is: you are NOT your anger. You are NOT that experience. He can be VERY VERY powerful, practically possessing your body with a strong emotion that is unlike the other saboteurs in the way he blinds your senses and decision making processes. The ability for you to become a master of your Angry Android is to practice, practice, practice being aware, being a witness, being an observer of his behavior in you and in others. The LESS energy you give to him, the less frequent he will be successful in derailing you from a positive state of mind and the train of thought for you to remain happy.

THE GUILT GHOST

The Guilt Ghost really doesn't have to work very hard to render you powerless. He has been known to cause you to collapse in despair and self-loathing, and then stands there chuckling. The Guilt Ghost is a nothing but a coward.

He only stands behind you. He'll poke you in the back and whisper things in your ear. Constantly hovering, he slips away, ducks behind you again, or hides out of sight. His behavior is slippery. The Guilt Ghost knows how to push your buttons, and is especially good at getting an emotional rise out of you. He's good at what he does. It's almost too easy.

In a couple of seconds, you can be completely derailed by a Guilt Ghost. That's because he knows how readily you will take the blame, admit a mistake and take credit for failure. He knows that you'll take the blame for something you didn't even do! In this way, he is ruthless. He lies about something being your fault and then he laughs behind your back as you hold your head in shame.

Sometimes the Guilt Ghost doesn't have to lie. He can smell your secrets and it is his job to turn them into a weapon against you. He knows the mere mention of the word "mistake" or "failure" from the Guilt Ghost usually gets a rise out of you.

THE VEIL

Guilt creates a feeling of being all tangled up in shame. That's why the baggage of the Guilt Ghost is the Veil because the Guilt Ghost wants you to hide your head in shame. The continuous replaying of mental sound bites of shameful or embarrassing events from your past cause you to hide from the world.

The Veil is a thin layer that blurs your vision, and keeps you from feeling worthy of being seen and heard. Embarrassment is the experience of caving internally. You feel hunched over, only will to face the ground so you don't have to make eye contact with anyone and risk any further shame.

Because the Guilt Ghost exploits your past mistakes through sneering, or taunting reminders of your moments of humiliation, he provides you this Veil to remind you to stay in a state of shame.

HOW TO RESPOND

The Guilt Ghost aims to shame you. He aims to haunt you. Haunting is the act of being preyed upon. Being haunted can eventually cause crisis for you. So while he's one of the more powerful saboteurs and the more ruthless of them all, you must face him and look him in the eye. This may require you to face head on what it is you feel shame about.

When you're face to face with the Guilt Ghost, it can feel painful, sometimes even unbearable. This pain is emotional pain and it ends when it is officially dealt with. You can deal with it by your willingness to face it. You can face these memories by writing them down and looking at who you were at that time in the past. Remember guilt is an emotion associated with something that already happened. It's important to recognize that because of who you are today is not the same person as who you were yesterday. The Guilt Ghost often wants you to feel extreme shame in order for you to learn to forgive yourself.

Learning to forgive what you have done in the past, even if it was yesterday is a very important practice in being able to control your emotional states. You are always growing and learning each day. So if you feel guilty about something, make amends with yourself by promising to learn from your mistakes. If someone else is trying to make you feel ashamed, remember that their inner Guilt Ghost doesn't have to become yours. You do not have to allow someone else to give you a Veil and hide your head in shame because their inner Guilt Ghost has gotten the best of them and mistreated you. Facing the Guilt Ghost will cause him to vanish into thin air. In this way, he has lost power over you because you are onto his tactics that derail you.

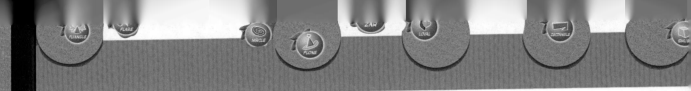

THE GREED FIEND

Deceit and manipulation are what motivates the Greed Fiend. He robs you slyly every which way and sideways. His offers are enticing and he talks really fast on purpose so you miss the scams and hidden information in his deals. If you aren't on your toes, you might find yourself nodding and agreeing without realizing what you're nodding and agreeing to. Be extremely careful! He'll tell you to sign on the dotted line with his hand over the fine print.

The Greed Fiend has the ability to see you coming a mile away. He has thought it all through and knows how to be persuasive. He knows exactly what he's going to say to you, when he's going to say it, and what he's going to say to every objection you make. He is the craftiest creature you will ever meet.

You may feel bewildered or taken for a ride after you leave him. You will realize that he took advantage of you because you weren't fully prepared for all his manipulation.

BUY

PASSES

Buy Passes are the baggage of the Greed Fiend because if the Greed Fiend succeeds, he has caused you to become hooked on some sort of suppressant. He has essentially succeeded in getting you to need him because he has become the source of your happiness. What he knows and always knew, was that the kind of happiness he offers is short lived. His tactic is to offer you something that you will feel pleasure from, only to find when the pleasure is gone, you are left with chronic hunger. He knows that your hunger will eventually make you desperate. He will then manipulate you more, as he follows up with a solution for you, however it's only temporary relief for whatever chronic hunger you have. This causes you to return time and time again to re-fill on whatever he's offering.

When the Greed Fiend shows up in you or someone else, he usually operates the same way: being very, very crafty. For instance, he shows up when you are suffering, in pain or uncomfortable. He first offers you a way out of your pain in a way that's hard to resist. He tells you he has "instant relief," and you will experience great pleasure that will carry into all aspects of your life such as help to improve your social life. Then, in your moment of weakness, he offers anything from something food related, to some form of drug or alcohol to something materialistic. He has many ideas depending on what state you are in!

Although they are instant, they problem with his methods is, without fail, result in some sort of major destruction in your life. His answers do not live up to what he has promised you will feel. The Greed Fiend doesn't care as long as you continue to return to him again and again.

HOW TO RESPOND

Say no. (Seems simple, but this can be most difficult for some of us.) The Greed Fiend is trying to make a "sale". Sometimes that comes in the form of convincing you of something, like selling you on an idea. For instance, someone's inner Greed Fiend can surface if he is trying to get people to agree with him to gain more power. Sometimes the Greed Fiend wants you to become addicted to something, and in these cases, the only way to respond to the Greed Fiend is by saying NO.

Being the good person you are, you may feel that saying no makes you are mean or rude. Are you worried about what the other person will think of you? One, saying no doesn't make you mean or rude! Two, who cares what a Greed Fiend thinks of you! The Greed Fiend makes it difficult to say no because he already plans for you to say no. He has prepared rebuttals for what happens if you say no, like how you will lose all your friends, or won't fit in, or how something will increase or decrease your popularity. He'll try to sell you something relentlessly, even resorting to insulting you if you don't say yes, or creating a scenario about how you are missing out. Just keep on saying no, over and over again because the only one who will advance by you giving into a Greed Fiend is the Greed Fiend.

The fact is, saying no simply is a signal to another person that they have crossed or are about to cross your personal boundaries. Personal boundaries are the invisible line or force field surrounding each person that mark your comfort zone and ultimately keep your safety in check. By letting other people know the boundaries of your comfort zone when those boundaries are crossed (by speaking up), you are showing you are willing to protect those boundaries. Sometimes you don't your boundaries UNTIL they are crossed. That's okay. That's how you learn. Once you learn yours, protect them.

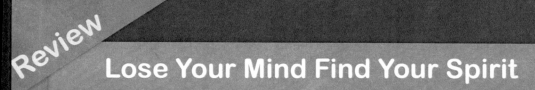

Lose Your Mind Find Your Spirit

When you become more conscious, the mind's fear based tricks lose their power and can't derail you easily. Follow your train of thought and you will discover your own unique Spirit.

Spirit

the nonphysical part of a person
that is the seat of emotions
and character
the "soul"

talent

focus

smarts

attitude

CHARACTER   FEAR VOICES

DECISIONS BEHAVIOR CHOICES

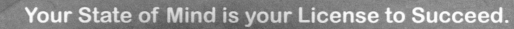

Your State of Mind is your License to Succeed.

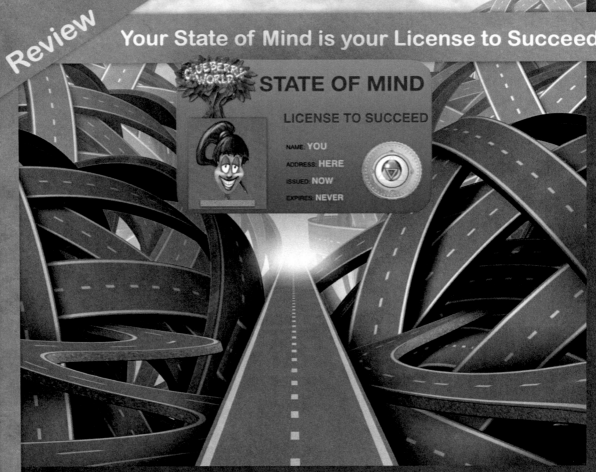

STATE OF MIND

LICENSE TO SUCCEED

NAME: **YOU**

ADDRESS: **HERE**

ISSUED: **NOW**

EXPIRES: **NEVER**

Life is a journey we learn to navigate. With so many distractions, options, voices, opinions, noise, avenues, ideas, paths, influences, what criteria do we choose to make a decision on which way is the best way? Clueberry World suggests turning inward and relying on your internal Clarity Compass to find your way. Once your mind is quiet, the inner voice that intuitively knows what's best for you will release one or more of the 8 kinds of Clueberries to guide you: Mircle (miracle or inspired thought), Flone (detachment), Shube (perspective), Zar (creativity), Zectangle (clarity), Fliangle (intuition), Loval (intention) and Flare (insight). Follow the Clueberries.

Summary

Go higher. Rise above what sabotages you!

Finding our way out of chaos is the process of becoming aware of negative thought forms sabotaging us but many don't realize...

The next step is to STEP INTO a new conditioning, a state of accepting and receiving excellence as the new normal. Fighting what we are now aware of as negative is a trick to keep us from moving forward.

The object of the game is now to claim, say yes to and follow empowered thoughts, fresh ideas, bright visions rather than stay fighting the old.

TIP: Any notion of unworthiness to pursue a new path is a last ditch effort of the thought system from the past to survive. It's the clueberry saboteurs yelling at you from their chaos to "'come back!' come back!' Fight with us!" AFFIRM: IT'S TIME FOR ME TO TAKE OFF.

ABOUT THE AUTHOR

Chrissy Harmon, M.Ed.
chrissyjane@gmail.com
www.clueberryworld.org

I created the first version of this book in 2008, after seeing a big problem in my 7th grade English Language Arts classroom. There was a need for a curriculum on fear, self sabotage and developing positive habits of mind. It had to be empowering yet fun. Clueberry World has grown since then into related products.
Thanks for reading,
Much love,
Chrissy

Made in the USA
Middletown, DE
12 December 2015